MICHELIN

TUSCANY

—in your pocket—

PHOTOGRAPH CREDITS

Travel Library 9; Travel Library/Daniel Cilia title page, 29; Travel Library/Citalia 47, 67, 69, 71, 112; Travel Library/Philip Enticknap front and back cover, title page, 5, 7, 10-11, 13, 16, 17, 18, 22, 23, 24-25, 27, 30, 31, 32, 33, 34, 35 (bottom), 36, 37, 38, 39 (top, bottom), 41, 43, 45, 48, 49, 50, 51, 53, 54, 55, 56, 58, 61, 65 (top, bottom), 73, 75 (top), 77, 79, 81, 83, 86, 88, 93, 96, 98, 99, 100, 102, 103, 105, 107, 109, 111, 115, 117, 121, 122, 124; Travel Library/John Welburn 97; Bridgeman Art Library 14, 15, 35 (top); Greg Evans International Photolibrary 95; Natural Image/Bob Gibbons 85; Natural Image/Peter Wilson 8, 66, 74.

Front cover: Tuscan hill town; back cover: copy of Michelangelo's David, in front of the Palazzo Vecchio, Florence; title page: view of Ponte Vecchio, Florence

MANUFACTURE FRANÇAISE DES PNEUMATIQUES MICHELIN

Société en commandite par actions au capital de 2 000 000 000 de francs

Place des Carmes-Déchaux – 63 Clermont-Ferrand (France)

R.C.S. Clermont-Fd 855 200 507

© Michelin et Cie. Propriétaires-Éditeurs 1996

Dêpôt légal Avril 96 – ISBN 2-06-650801-2– ISSN en cours

Printed in the EU 3-96

CONTENTS

INTRODUCTION

'Tuscany is art and commerce, Ceres and Bacchus, town and country, all in harmony.'

Asked to name a major city in Italy, people will invariably come up with Rome, Milan, Venice, Naples – and Florence. If asked to name the best known region, however, the likelihood is that the province of Tuscany will be the first to spring to mind.

This lovely part of Italy has been impressing the world for many centuries. In medieval times, it was a centre for business. With rich natural resources, the province built itself up as a focus of fashion and new ideas. Medieval Tuscans travelled extensively and had posts in many northern European cities, where they controlled trade in goods ranging from wool to wine.

Yet what impresses us still, perhaps because we possess so many riches from that time, is the artistic energy of this part of Italy. It culminated in that explosion of creativity, the Renaissance, which flowered in Florence five and a half centuries ago. The great works of art and architecture, centred in Florence and the surrounding Tuscan towns, still prove an enormous attraction for visitors.

Add to these the many historic remains, the castles and the churches, both chaste and over-dressed, the lovely and often un-changed city centres, wonderful countryside that constantly alters, food and wine that is memorable, and a proud, elegant and hospitable people, and you have a region that for many has no equal. The atmosphere of Tuscany, even in hot and windless summers, can convert a first-time visitor into one who returns many times, always to make fresh discoveries on each new visit. Tuscany is, to employ an over-indulged word, unique. Beware the allure of the part of Italy known as La Toscana – for this part of Italy is as much a state of mind as a physical place.

A winding trail of cypress trees stretches lazily across the rolling Tuscan hills.

HOW TO USE THIS GUIDE

This guide is divided into four main sections:

Background sets the scene, with an introduction to Tuscany's geography and landscape, an outline of its rich history, art, legends and heroes, and the culture and people of Tuscany today.

Exploring Tuscany starts with a list of the top sights which should be on everyone's holiday checklist. The reader is taken on a tour of Florence, the heart of Tuscany, taking in all the great art treasures, buildings, museums and sights. The main towns of the region are described, and there are special sections on mountains and hill towns, beaches and coastal resorts, the islands, terme, and holidaying with children in Tuscany, all with plenty of ideas for excursions and sightseeing.

Enjoying your visit provides friendly, no-nonsense advice on day-to-day holiday activities which can make the difference between a good aholiday and a great one – eating out, shopping, sports, entertainment and nightlife, as well as information about local festivals and the all-important factor – the weather.

A-Z Factfinder is an easy-to-use reference section packed with useful information, covering everything you may need to know, from tipping to hiring cars, from using the telephone to vaccinations.
A word of warning: opening hours and telephone numbers frequently change, so be sure to double check with a local tourist office when planning your visit.

The breathtaking views across Florence from the top of Giotto's Bell Tower are well worth the 82m (270ft) climb. You can also go to the top of Brunelleschi's great dome on the Cathedral, with equally spectacular views.

GEOGRAPHY

The Italian peninsula is in part a land of fiery origins as it is on the edge of a volcanic fault. Volcanoes, built up by lava forced from beneath the earth's crust, still exist in Italy (Vesuvius, Etna and Stromboli). In Tuscany, however, they are long dead, though still physically present in the form of volcanic plugs and mountains like Monte Amiata. These sudden hills, often capped with medieval towns, mark ancient volcanic activity.

Tuscany spreads east from the Mediterranean shore, while the sea (known as the Tyrrhenian Sea) is dotted with Tuscan islands between the mainland and Corsica, the largest being Elba. The region, shaped like a triangle, is bounded on the north-east by the Apennines, on the west by the Tyrrhenian Sea and to the south by a complex of mountains, valleys and plains.

The Apuan Alps are the source of some of the finest marble in the world, which has been extracted since Roman times from quarries like these at Carrara.

The Tyrrhenian coastline, formed from the seabed forced up into mountains of hard-pressed limestone, is rocky to the south of Leghorn, contrasting with the long stretches of white sandy beaches to the north-west, known as the Versilia. To the north of Tuscany, the heavily-wooded Apuan Alps are quarried for the fine marble for which Italy has long been famous. Different again is the south-western coastal plain of Maremma – an area of marshland now largely reclaimed, which has Etruscan sites and museums and a haunting beauty which hints at its mysterious past when it was only inhabited by bandits and shepherds.

The heart of Tuscany is the Arno Basin, a rich and fertile area stretching from Florence to Siena, which forms the centre of the Chianti vine- and olive-growing region. The volcanic outpourings have led to very fertile soils, which have been deposited in the river valleys that wind down from the

Netting threaded between the trees of an olive grove, ready to be unfurled during harvesting.

central comb of the Apennine range on the eastern edges. Narrow at first, the valleys open out into wide areas of vineyards and agricultural land, abundant with fruits and vegetables, and plenty of fodder for the livestock, particularly the big white cattle.

The general impression of Tuscany is of a

Agriculture has always been important in Tuscany, with vineyards and other crops flourishing on the rich soils.

green, hilly land of woods and pasture, well-watered and productive. It does, however, have wild, mysterious parts: deep-cut valleys bounded by craggy hills, and marshes like the Maremma, a landscape which the Roman imagination populated with satyrs and other dark gods.

BACKGROUND

HISTORY

You cannot avoid history in Tuscany. It is
everywhere: from ancient burial grounds to
medieval hill towns, from gorgeously
frescoed churches to a parade of palaces. Yet
in this part of Italy, history is not something
set apart; it is vital, ongoing in the life of the
people. You can see it in the pleasure they
take in their buildings, squares and gardens,
in the throngs of local folk at museums
when there are 'free days' (usually Sundays).
Here, history is a living thing.

Early origins and the Etruscans

Indeed, there is history in the very name
Tuscany – the word comes from the original
inhabitants, the mysterious Etruscans. Early
evidence of prehistoric man is recorded at
Cetona, near Chiusi, and in Pontremoli's
Museum, while fossils dating from even
earlier can be seen at Montevarchi's
Accademia. Yet it is the Etruscans which
Tuscans regard as their ancestors.

The **Etruscans** arrived from the 8C BC and
set up a nation state, ruled by twelve cities.
Although they lived and flourished for some
five centuries before Rome was an Imperial
city, tantalizingly little is known of these
cultivated people. Much of the remaining
Etruscan art which survived the subsequent
Roman domination is in the form of grave
goods and tombs. You can see Etruscan
remains in Florence and in regional
museums such as those at Chiusi, Cortona,
Volterra and Grosseto. There are extensive
tombs at Populonia, Sorano, Sovana and
Vetulonia.

Romans

The Romans absorbed the Etruscan race and culture from about 280 BC. While the Etruscans' presence in Tuscany has shaped the country and people, we find there today, the Romans too have left their mark. Remains can be found in places such as Ansedonia, Fiesole, Lucca, Montalcino and Roselle. Ancient Rome is never far away; indeed, it is under the very stones you walk on, for Florence conceals Roman ruins, the

The remains of a Roman temple at Fiesole.

city being founded by **Julius Caesar** in 59 BC.
There are also impressive villas, such as
those at **Ansedonia** and the **Isle of
Giannutri**, while amphitheatres can be seen
at **Fiesole**, **Lucca**, **Arezzo** and **Volterra**.

Tuscany remained under Roman control
until the Empire collapsed in AD 476. An era
of struggle and decline ensued as Goths and
Lombards invaded, all eager to possess a
region rich in natural resources. Finally,
Tuscany came under the rule of
Charlemagne in AD 774.

*The Madonna, by
Giotto, painted in
c. 1310 – just one
of the treasures in
the Uffizi Gallery,
Florence.*

There followed a turbulent period of rivalry between the **Ghibellines** supporting the emperor and the **Guelphs** supporting the pope. As new towns rose, fortifications and castles were constructed, and many imposing civic palaces were built.

Renaissance

In the medieval period, Tuscany was a series of small but powerful fiefdoms, constantly battling with each other. Yet this bloody time in the region's history parallels an eruption of the arts and the birth of some of the greatest artists the world has ever known. The period from the 13C to the 16C was one in which intellectual and artistic excellence flourished in a way unrivalled anywhere else. The period, known as the **Renaissance**, was to affect the cultural development not only of Italy, but of Europe too.

Renaissance means 'rebirth', and Tuscany produced, in a few glorious decades, an

Sandro Botticelli's The Birth of Venus (c. 1485), in the Uffizi Gallery, Florence.

abundance of brilliant blooms from artists such as Botticelli, della Robbia, Donatello, della Francesca, Giotto, Ghiberti, da Vinci, Masaccio and Michelangelo, to name but a few. Musicians, sculptors, architects, writers and poets were among the greatest history has seen.

Conditions were right for this important rebirth in the 15C, as the new culture exploded. The Renaissance was fuelled by fashion, by the wish to aggrandize, and by money. The artists needed patronage to pay for the simple business of living. Their patrons were merchants, aristocrats and, most importantly, the Church.

Right Ammannati's imposing Fountain of Neptune is just one of the statues which adorn the Piazza della Signoria, Florence.

Below In Florence's Medici Chapels are the famous Medici tombs, by Michelangelo.

The art of Siena flowered before the Renaissance, with whole shoals of piquant pictures of saints and martyrs. A great rival to Florence, Siena fostered artists such as Duccio di Boninsegna, Simone Martini, Guido da Siena, Beccafumi and Sodoma. But Florence was the main driving force of the movement, and influenced neighbouring towns which responded in rivalry. The first family of Florence, the **Medici**, commissioned works to adorn palaces, galleries, even gardens. This new, enlightened attitude to culture was cultivated by followers, providing a fertile pool of patronage. The money and patronage of the ruling classes pushed Tuscany, and particularly Florence, to new artistic and intellectual heights, making it a model for Italy, and the rest of Europe too.

Dante, the 13C poet, wrote his epic poem the Divine Comedy in Tuscan dialect. He is commemorated at this reconstruction of his home in Florence. This shows the bust outside the house.

Wealth from a variety of trades, from wool to wine, banking to bookeeping, had produced a new level of society wishing to decorate castles, churches, public buildings, palaces and, as at last life grew more secure, their country villas.

There already existed a heritage of fine medieval buildings but the newly-powerful developed an insatiable appetite for furnishing their homes sumptuously and surrounding themselves with new and beautiful objects. This produced a surge not just in architecture and the visual arts, but in music, writing and poetry, bringing Dante, the father of the Italian language, Petrarch, Boccaccio and many minor poets to the fore. Artists were called upon to supply a variety of works, from pictures sacred and profane, to garden designs. Elaborate entertainments were given, needing writers, designers and musicians.

The impact of the Renaissance was felt – and can still be seen – throughout the Western world. But the finest works of art are to be found in the many museums of Tuscany – even in small towns and villages. The heart of the Renaissance was in Florence. Five hundred years on, we see the life of the city and her neighbours reflected in the works of sublime artists.

Modern Italy

The Medici declined in the 18C. A hundred years later, in 1860, during the Unification of Italy, Tuscany was incorporated in a new and modern state, unified for the first time since the Romans, yet retaining the liveliness and individuality of its many parts.

The Mysterious Etruscans

There are few peoples more mysterious than the Etruscans. As we see them now in their elegant, sculpted tomb figures, they seem quiet, quizzical, remote. Little is known of this tribe of people who lived in Tuscany from 800 BC until the Roman armies subdued and changed them from 280 BC onwards. Yet their cities and settlements were widespread throughout present-day Tuscany and extended into neighbouring areas. They left behind impressive monuments and tombs around their cities, such as Cortona, Arezzo, Fiesole, Chiusi and Volterra.

In many Tuscan museums you will find glimpses of the lifestyle of the ancient Etruscans. In vases and pots, as well as their spectacular red stone tomb statuary, in jewellery and ornaments, the handsome race emerges as a people with well-defined, sophisticated tastes and a unique culture.

There is much we do not know about the Etruscans, partly because many of their artefacts and cities were made of wood and have not survived, and also because the Romans integrated the race and its culture so effectively. Most of the evidence of their social organization and their lifestyle comes from the many tombs which are found all over Tuscany, with the grandest found in the south, such as Cerveteri and Tarquinia. Built near their hill-top cities, the huge burial grounds consist of under-ground chambers filled with artefacts and with paintings. These reflect the joys of living – eating and drinking, dancing and music, hunting and so on – and give us an insight of what life was like.

If you wish to do some research before you go to Italy, read about these people and look at their arts. When you arrive, you will find much sculpture and tomb decora-tions preserved at the sites, while many museums contain Etruscan finds.

Some say you can still feel the Etruscan presence in the land that was once theirs. Certainly you can sense their individuality in the proud cities they built, which preserve Etruscan walls, habitations and tombs. And their name lingers on in the word 'Tuscan', a relic of the lost land of Etruria.

The famous sculpture of the Chimera, from Arezzo, can be seen in Florence's Archaeological Museum.

PEOPLE AND CULTURE

Appropriately for an ancient land, occupied by a civilized people for over 3 000 years, many of its present-day residents claim descent from Etruscans or Romans. Certainly, the people here often have an elegant, classical appearance and a sense of belonging to their region. Whether Etruscan looks do linger on is anyone's guess. It is interesting to speculate as you look at Etruscan sculptures and pictorial busts in museums such as those at Chiusi, or Volterra, where many claim Etruscan blood, or in Florence's fine Etruscan collection.

Look at Tuscans on the street. It is always hard to make generalizations, yet as they walk in piazzas or shop in open markets, there is real evidence of a Tuscan character. They are lively, a smooth-skinned people, often dark, with generous mouths, tall and with character. An attractive people, whatever the age.

Discussions can become quite animated, but are usually good-natured.

Politeness is instinctive, too, and that mysterious quality – charm – though not peculiar to Tuscany, is often evident when you meet and talk. They appreciate being told that you enjoy their towns and their country, their way of life. If you acquire some Italian – even if only a few halting words – here, where the roots of the modern language were established by the illustrious Dante, you will be encouraged with smiles and compliments. Indeed, their language is a pleasure to listen to, often spoken rapidly, yet clearly, accompanied with much body-language ranging from shrugs to bold and dramatic gesticulations.

Throughout Italy, street life is important – warm evenings in piazzas or main streets go on into the night, as residents visit and chat over outdoor meals or at café tables. It is courtship time for the young, children are paraded, old people sit over coffee or grappa – and are not forgotten in the age-old social display. Small wonder, then, that for centuries the sociable atmosphere so common here has drawn many foreigners to visit (and sometimes never leave) seductive Tuscany.

There is always time to sit and pass the time of day.

MUST SEE

It is very hard in such a rich part of the world to choose ten top spots – and inevitably you will find your own favourites, often small and secret ones. Here, however, is a list of ten attractions you should not miss.

Florence
This undoubtedly comes at the top of the list. Home to many world renowned works of art, Florence remains one of the most extraor-

dinarily culturally rich cities in the world.

Siena
A spectacular little city, tightly folded into the hills, with a magnificent shell-shaped piazza at its heart.

Pisa
The Leaning Tower is only part of a magnificent group of buildings in the Campo dei Miracoli, in this once great rival to Florence.

The terraces of the Boboli Gardens offer superb panoramic views of Florence and the countryside beyond.

Elba
Napoleon's island, this is a place of seductive beauty with mountains and beaches, and good swimming in the clear warm waters.

San Gimignano
With warring families building tall towers to defend themselves, the town preserves something of the look it had when there were dozens of these eccentric constructions.

There are quiet, unspoilt hill towns such as Pereta, waiting to be explored.

Mountains
A day in the Apennines, exploring the stony spine of Italy, is memorable indeed. You will get away from the crowds and also appreciate the modern engineering marvels of the autostrade, high-striding through the steep ravines.

The Chianti Route
Get off the highway and follow the well-marked Chianti Route that dips into the wine country along the rural roads south of Florence. Stop, taste and picnic!

Monte Argentario
Here you have the best of contrasting landscapes – a mountainous isle almost surrounded by sea, with fine beaches and excellent swimming. Good seafood, too!

Typical Hill Town
There are many of these to choose from. Try Pienza, whose town square was the first example of Renaissance town planning; Monteriggioni, with a complete circle of towers and walls; mysterious Sovana, with its Etruscan tombs; or Certaldo, built of rosy brick, where Boccaccio spent his last years.

Medieval Sports and Games
If you visit towns such as Siena, Arezzo,
Sansepolcro or Montepulciano, you can see
the colourful and dramatic re-enactments of
old customs and festivals (*see also* pp.40-41).

FLORENCE

Tuscany's essence is contained within its capital Florence, *Firenze*, the 'city of flowers'. This sophisticated and elegant city offers an almost endless series of magical experiences, as one explores the museums, churches, galleries and sights of what is often called

The evening light brings out the rich colours of Florence's oldest bridge, the Ponte Vecchio.

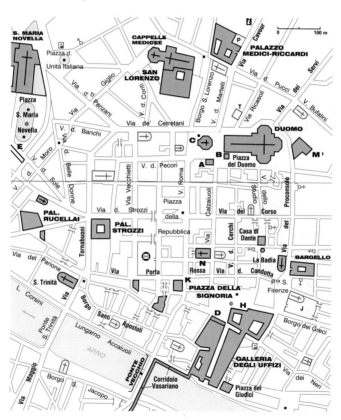

'The Capital of the Arts'.

It is no small wonder that the city, founded by **Julius Caesar** on the winding River Arno, spanned by the famous **Ponte Vecchio**, is one of the most popular attractions in Italy. As the main sights are quite close together, it is best explored on foot; the compact centre is car-free, though crowded in summer, so try to visit in spring or early autumn.

Main buildings

The **Cathedral (Duomo) of Santa Maria del Fiore** is visually stunning, not only because of its sheer size (it is one of the largest in the Christian world) but because of the vivid colours of marble used in its exterior decoration (red from the Maremma, green from Prato and, of course, white from

Map of Florence
Key
A *Loggia del Bigallo*
B *Campanile*
C *Battistero*
H *Palazzo Vecchio*
M¹ *Museo dell' Opera del Duomo*
D *Loggia dei Lanzi*
E *Loggia di San Paolo*
K *Mercato Nuovo*
N *Orsanmichele*

The Cathedral, Bell Tower and Baptistery – clad in white, green and red marble – form the heart of the city.

Carrara). Begun in 1296, it was finally completed only in 1463, after some 14 years spent on the problematic dome. The splendid result that we see today was achieved by **Brunelleschi**, using a cantilevered construction to bear the great weight and, despite the sceptics of the time, it worked. You can go up to the top of the dome (if you have the energy and a good head for heights) where you will see one of the best panoramas of Florence. The current facade dates from the 19C. The interior is comparatively unadorned and sombre, but the immense size is impressive, and there are some worthy frescoes and works of art.

Mosaics adorning the interior of the Baptistery dome depict the Last Judgement.

The octagonal **Baptistery** (Battistero San Giovanni) has the oldest origins in Florence,

being built on Roman foundations. The three sets of bronze doors are famous, and rightly so, for set against the white and green marble exterior, they are truly magnificent. There were competitions among the leading artists of the time to see who would design each pair. The South Doors are by **Andrea Pisano** and show scenes of John the Baptist and the Virtues. The North Doors, by **Lorenzo Ghiberti**, show scenes from the life of Christ, while in the East Doors (which took 27 years to complete) he shows scenes from the Old Testament. Michelangelo described these as the 'Gate to Paradise'.

Giotto's Bell Tower (Campanile di Giotto), another construction in different coloured marbles, crafted in vivid geometric

The bronze doors of the Baptistery are, quite rightly, world famous and always attract a large crowd of visitors.

design, is equally striking, and counter-balances the dome perfectly. There is a panoramic view from the top of this 82m (270ft) tower.

Museums

While in the area, you should visit the **Cathedral Museum** (Museo dell'Opera del Duomo) which houses items from the Cathedral, Tower and Baptistery. There is **Michelangelo**'s *Pietà*, the original panels from the Baptistery East Doors, **Brunelleschi**'s death mask and **Donatello** sculptures.

Palazzo Vecchio has been the home of the Florentine government since 1299. A majestic, but somewhat severe-looking

The lavish splendour of the Renaissance interior of the Palazzo Vecchio contrasts with its solid and severe Gothic exterior, dominated by its tall tower.

building, it is topped by a tall, slender tower (94m/310ft), housing a famous bell, *La Vacca* (The Cow). The interior, in contrast, is pure Renaissance, lavishly decorated and adorned with wonderful sculptures and works of art. In the **Loggia dei Lanzi**, beside the Palazzo Vecchio, are sculptures such as **Giambologna**'s *Rape of the Sabine* and **Cellini**'s *Perseus*, facing reproductions of other famous works across the beautiful wide piazza, including a copy of Michelangelo's *David*.

Florence has some of the finest museums in Europe, ranging from the excellent to the sublime. The greatest is the

The Rape of the Sabine (1583), in the Loggia dei Lanzi.

Uffizi Gallery (Galleria degli Uffizi) housed in a Renaissance palace designed by **Vasari**. Containing perhaps the best single collection of Florentine paintings, as well as a wide range of fine works from other eras and countries, you have to be selective, using the museum guidebook to plan your visit. You will have to choose between the works of Michelangelo, Titian, Caravaggio, Giotto, Simone Martini, Piero della Francesca, Uccello, Filippo Lippi, Sandro Botticelli, Hugo van der Goes, Verrocchio, Leonardo da Vinci, Raphael and many more.

The **Academy Gallery** (Galleria dell'Accademia) is a must, even if you only see

Portrait of the beautiful Lucrezia Panciatichi, by Agnolo Bronzino (Uffizi Gallery).

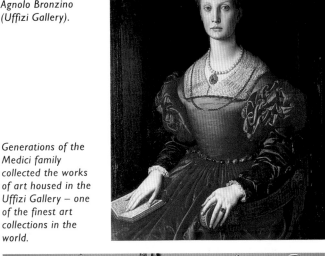

Generations of the Medici family collected the works of art housed in the Uffizi Gallery – one of the finest art collections in the world.

Michelangelo's *David* and the *Four Slaves*.

There are numerous other museums, such as the **Archaeological Museum** (Museo Archeologico) with a vast collection of Greek, Roman, Egyptian and Etruscan works, and the **Museum of Florence As it Was** (Museo di Firenze Com'era), which traces the history of Florence through maps, drawings and plans. How many of these you

The original of Michelangelo's David is housed in the Academy Gallery.

The terraced Boboli Gardens offer a peaceful haven in which to rest between visits to the Pitti Palace's six museums and galleries.

visit will depend upon the time available, but one that should not be missed is the **Bargello Palace and Museum**. Rather stern and austere, this one-time prison houses important works by **Donatello** and **Michelangelo**.

Palaces

In the palaces of Florence there are more marvels. The **Pitti Palace** is set in the **Boboli Gardens**. The most atypical of the Florentine palaces, it is imposing but almost like a fortress. It houses many works of art, arranged in six museums and art galleries, the most significant being the **Palatine Gallery** (Galleria Palatina) with works by **Raphael**, **Titian** and many more, all set in the beautiful rooms, adorned with frescoes and wall paintings. You need separate tickets for each of the museums and galleries, so it can be expensive to visit several of them.

Other palaces, such as the **Medici Palace** (Palazzo Medici-Riccardi), offer different treats – a **Gozzoli** procession gleams from chapel walls as the Magi march by. In the **Palazzo Davanzati** you are invited into a medieval household which has the appearance of still being lived in. At the **Palazzos Strozzi** and **Gondi** there are splendid courtyards. Some palaces are used as centres for social, art and antique trade events.

Churches

Many of the churches are galleries in themselves. **Santa Croce** has a pantheon of tombs and frescoes showing style changes, through Giotto to the Renaissance. **San Lorenzo** shows Michelangelo's languid, yet mesmerising tomb figures and his Laurenziana Library, as well as pulpits by Donatello. The convent of **San Marco** has Fra Angelicos. **Santa Maria Novella** has many

Frescoes in the Capella Medicee, attached to San Lorenzo.

This mosaic in the Apse of San Miniato depicts Christ blessing the Virgin.

fine frescoes, including those by Ghirlandaio and Masaccio, and paintings by Giotto, Orcagna and Bronzino, while astride its hill **San Miniato**'s enticing facade beckons you up the long climb to the rewards of a glorious, cool interior and crypt, della Robbias and a room of frescoes by Spinello Aretino. Afterwards, visit the **Vescovi Palace** next door, now a concert hall, or rest on the terrace for a panoramic view of the city – recompense for all the effort!

After all the sightseeing, a sit down and drink is welcome – especially when the table commands such views.

Medieval Games and Events

Imagine being transported back to the 14C in a setting that already recaptures history. In Tuscany, you can actually do just that, for every year whole towns turn out with costumes, weapons, and even lights and music to recreate medieval events. You can feel part of it when you attend festivals and recreations of games and pastimes.

In Italy's old towns, the sense of living history all around you is reinforced by the very real enthusiasm of the local people. On these special occasions, they love dressing up to recall an historic event or an ancient ceremony. This is true not only of early spring carnivals, but also of the many medieval games that are re-enacted in the centres of old towns, usually in summer or early autumn. Events range from the famous **Palio of Siena** (a horse race around the campo, with ten riders chosen from 17 sections of the city), to the **Joust of the Saracen** in the piazza of **Arezzo** – a spectacular medieval-style joust which follows the colourful parade

to the piazza. Other places offering such attractions include **Sansepolcro** with a show of crossbows, re-enacting the dispute between the marksmen of Sansepolcro and Gubbio, in Umbria. **Massa Marittima** also has crossbow displays. **Montepulciano** re-enacts the town's history in the Bruscello, with an open-air banquet after a colourful

procession and barrel race – the Bravío delle Botti.

Although commercially-inspired, some towns have equally interesting annual fairs, such as the horse and wine fiera di San Luca in **Impruneta**, or the Chianti fair held every May in **Pontassieve**, or **Lari**'s celebrations of the fruit harvest.

In addition, many towns hold pre-Lenten carnivals. **San Vicenzo** has a large commer-cial show designed to attract out-of-season visitors, but smaller places often have a local event, complete with masked revellers and dances, such as the one at **Bibbiena**, with its bello ballo dance at the end of the carnival. Note, however, that events usually only take place once a year, and sometimes not as often as that, so check first with the Italian tourist office.

Procession before the Calcio medieval football, Florence.

EXPLORING TUSCANY

TOWNS AND CITIES

Surely no other place on earth has so many settlements of such diversity, antiquity and charisma clustered so close together? Tuscany's intriguing towns pepper the region, from sun-facing beach resorts to hill-top towns and villages. Do not be put off by new unsightly development on the outskirts of some towns and cities, as the urban centres remain unchanged and strictly preserved. Most are traffic-free, making exploring on foot a more enjoyable experience.

Arezzo

Musicians know this small city from **Guido Monaco**, who invented the musical scale. Arezzo, in fact, is associated with a whole roster of names, from **Petrarch** to the writer/artists **Aretino** and **Vasari**. Although old Arezzo, set on a hillside, is surrounded with a circlet of modern suburbs, it remains a gem with many elegant palazzi, notably **Piazza Grande**, and churches, including the lovely Romanesque **Pieve di Santa Maria**, whose many-windowed campanile looms like an exclamation mark over the town. The famous frescoes by **Piero della Francesca** can be seen in the choir of **St Francis' Church** (San Francesco).

There is a 1C BC Roman amphitheatre and the **Archaeological Museum** (Museo Archeologico) featuring the renowned Roman red-coral coloured pottery. The city's business is based on agriculture and with its situation at the eastern rim of Tuscany, it is essentially rural; all in all, Arezzo makes a fine centre for exploring nearby towns and country.

The campanile of the Pieve di Santa Maria towers over the rooftops of Arezzo.

Carrara

Strange to reflect that marble, a brilliant hard limestone in a variety of colours and veining, owes its existence to minuscule sea creatures whose shells, or chalky skeletal structures, dead and down-drifting over the millennia, formed a blanket of sea-bottom sludge. Later, after undergoing immense heat and pressure, this sea-cemetery was pushed up to form mountains. The 300 or more quarries of the Apuan Alps reputedly hold the highest quality white marble in the world. You can visit the quarries, which produce 500 000 tons annually, and see the gleaming marble blocks in the railyard as trains roll past Marina di Carrara. There is an open-air museum at **Fantiscritti**. Much marble is destined for exotic bathrooms, but sculptors still come here to choose pieces, just as **Michelangelo** did. His famous *David* in the Accademia in Florence was created from a flawed block from here.

Carrara is not all marble, however. Although not noted as a tourist town, worth seeing, too, are the pink baroque palaces, a part-Romanesque cathedral with a fine framed rose window, a 16C fountain and, not least, a 19C opera house.

Chiusi – south of Arezzo

This small town is a must if you are intrigued by the Etruscans, as it was one of the 12 sovereign cities of Etruria. Set on a hill in the south-east of Etruria, its relative proximity to Rome meant it fell early. There are many Etruscan tombs to be viewed, and a mystery one – that of **Lars Porsenna**, a king who defied Rome and whose legendary tomb, surrounded by a maze, has never been found. The **Etruscan Museum** (Museo Etrusco) is by the cathedral, which itself is full of Etruscan stones and Roman columns, the result of quarrying and recycling local ruins a thousand years later. There are many Etruscan passages under the town.

Cortona – south of Arezzo

Secret Tuscany can still be found. On the borders of Umbria, set amid vineyards and olive groves, Cortona stands on a ridge of the Apennines, surrounded by fortifications, tombs and other traces of Etruria. Cortona

To walk through Cortona's medieval streets is to step back in time.

is a centre for many works of art; the **Palazzo Casali** has a range of Etruscan sculptures. There are several fine churches, notably the **duomo** (originally Romanesque but remodelled), **Santa Maria del Calcinaio** and **Santa Maria Nuova**. In the **Diocesan Museum** (Museo Diocesano) is the beautiful **Madonna and Saints** by **Fra Angelico**, and more paintings by **Signorelli**. There are many palaces. Prominent above the ramparts, with wide views of the country, is the **Medicea fort** (Fortezza Medicea).

Elba

This large island is most attractive when approached from the sea, and its beauty is revealed further once you land and begin to discover this lovely island of woods and mountains.

Elba's name resounded throughout a relieved Europe as the place where **Napoleon** was incarcerated from 1814 to 1815. Although considered safely put away, a mere ten months later he had escaped to France, only to re-activate his ambitions, leading to Waterloo and a second banishment, this time on the lonely St Helena. There is a small museum in his town house, the **Napoleonic Museum** (Villa dei Mulini). You can also visit his modest summer residence in **San Martino**. Napoleon's presence has meant that Elba's Etruscan and Roman history, sites and museums, are often overlooked.

The island is very busy in the summer months, so try to visit in spring or autumn. You will find verdant country, sailing, swimming, and many sandy beaches in the lovely bays. Elba has its share of development, but as new projects are controlled, it has retained its essential charm. In summer, escape the heat by going inland, where there are small villages and a yellow chair-lift from **Marciana** will carry you up **Monte Capanne** for extensive views of the island and across to the mainland.

Seafood abounds, but there is a local sweet which is also worth trying. **Scacciabriaca** comes from *scacciare* (to squash), a cake made with local fruits and flours, pushed into a pan and baked flat. Soaked in heavy red wine, this solid sweet is Arab in origin.

It is little wonder that the beautiful island of Elba is so popular.

These Roman baths at Fiesole were built in the 1C BC.

Fiesole – near Florence

Florence is old, but her near neighbour and one-time rival is even older. In this hill-top town, there are many Roman and Etruscan remains. The view of the countryside and Florence is spectacular from the **Monastery of St Francis** (San Francesco). At the **Archaeological Site** (Zona Archeologica) are Roman baths and a theatre and Etruscan temple walls, though the impressive temple housing the museum was built in this century. Fiesole boasts a fine **duomo** on the **Piazza Mino da Fiesole**, with some lovely sculptures. Most of Fiesole's churches have treasures. Nearby are many lovely villas, such as **Villa Medici**, **Michelozzo**'s 15C country house which, like so many great Italian houses, is privately owned.

Grosseto

Protected by a 16C rampart and bastions, now gardens, Grosseto is the capital of the low-lying marshy Maremma area, which was little visited until the last century because of the danger of malaria. It is an ideal base to explore the region's wildlife and history, as well as sample its produce, from snails and seafood to game and goat.

The martial turreted building on **Piazza Dante** is the small town hall, with the pink and white **duomo** next to it. Founded in the 13C, it is now much restored, but retains its elegance. There is a **Natural History Museum**, while the **Maremma Art and Archaeological Museum** (Museo Archeologico e d'Arte della Maremma) has a major collection, with Etruscan/Roman finds and early Sienese pictures. Nearby towns are the Etruscan **Roselle Scavi** and the Roman **Vetulonia**, both well worth a detour.

The flowing lines on this statue on the Piazza Dante, contrast with the turreted town hall of Grosseto.

Livorno (Leghorn)

Leghorn, as it was known to the English, probably because it was first developed as a harbour by the Elizabethan, Robert Dudley, is principal container port for Italy. Heavy bombardment in World War II meant devastated older sections were replaced, including the duomo, although the town maintains a good atmosphere. The **duomo** (portico by **Inigo Jones**) was rebuilt to an original plan. There are two fortresses: a moated one in the town, and the other in the harbour, with a large tower. The railway station is Art Nouveau. There are many excellent seafood restaurants around the old port (especially recommended are the shellfish and eels). Appropriately, there is an **aquarium** and a **marine research centre**. Famous names associated with Livorno include the composer **Mascagni**, and the painter **Modigliani**.

Lucca

A magical, and quite unspoilt town, Lucca possesses many treasures. Antiquity is everywhere, and the buildings are beautifully maintained. The town's origins as

The tree-lined promenade built on the 16C ramparts which encircle Lucca provides a shady walk with good views of this charming town. You can hire bicycles to ride round the walls – popular with children.

a Roman settlement, with the typical grid street plan, can still be detected through the complex overlay of narrow streets, alleys and squares that were added during the Middle Ages.

The wide promenade along the massive 16C walls is not to be missed: the 4km walk encircles the town. Early riches derived from banking and the silk trade in the 14C, and

The Piazza dell' Anfiteatro (also known as the Piazza Mercato) is built on the site of a Roman amphitheatre, mirroring its original shape.

later prosperity in the 16C, financed the building of the great civic treasures: the Romanesque **duomo**, the churches of **St Michael's** (San Michele) and **St Frigidian's** (San Frediano) with their fantastic facades, and the Renaissance palaces. The **Piazza dell' Anfiteatro** keeps the elliptical shape of the Roman amphitheatre it is built on. Worth a visit too is the town house of the **Guinigi** family, where you can climb the old clocktower, with its trees growing from the top, and experience wonderful views of the city and the surrounding countryside.

Lucca is a city to stay in and explore for several days, if you have time; there is so much to see, both within the city and just outside it. **Napoleon** gave Lucca to his sister, **Elisa**, in 1805, and she built a summer palace, **Villa Reale**, one of several grandiose country villas nearby. After Napoleon's downfall, Lucca was given as a duchy to **Marie-Louise de Bourbon**.

The splendid Madonna di San Biagio was completed in 1529. Designed in the shape of a Greek cross, and crowned with a dome, its architect Antonio da Sangallo was clearly influenced by St Peters in Rome.

Montepulciano – southwest of Siena

This long, hill town, perched on volcanic rocks, is crammed with fine buildings of every period. As you explore the traffic-free streets of this delightful town, take time to appreciate the outstanding **palaces** (ten, in all), such as the **Palazzo Nobili-Tarugi**, opposite the duomo. Many are the creation of **Sangallo**. The **Piazza Grande** is the heart of the town, with a town hall, a 16C **Cathedral** (look for the gold triptych altarpieces), an interesting well with griffons and lions, and the **Museum** (Museo Civico), housed in the **Neri-Orselli Palace**, which has a fine collection of terracotta, Etruscan remains and 13C-18C paintings.

Just beyond the town walls is **Sant'Agnese**,

with a frescoed cloister. To the south-west is
the **Madonna di San Biagio** – a 16C church
by Sangallo, set on a wooded hillside. The
church is built of warmly-coloured travertine
and the satisfyingly simple design set in such
beautiful surroundings makes it one of the
finest of its epoch.

The town has many special events and
parades (*see* p. 91).

Pisa

It is all too easy to regard Pisa as the city with the curious leaning tower, and nothing more. True, it is an impressive sight, but Pisa has many more splendours to offer the visitor with a little more time to explore. Of course, one must begin in the **Piazza del Duomo** (also called the **Campo dei Miracoli**), with its four wonders of architecture.

The **Cathedral** (Duomo), with its four-tiered facade, external decoration and use of coloured marbles to create geometric patterns, is a fine example of the **Pisan-Romanesque** style of architecture (do not miss the finely-carved **Giovanni Pisano** pulpit inside).

The **Leaning Tower** (Torre Pendente or

Set in the green lawns of the Campo dei Miracoli is the imposing and majestic dome of the Baptistery, with the Duomo and Tower of Pisa in the background.

Campanile) was begun in 1173 and completed in 1350. Made of white marble, the 58m tower is now leaning precariously as a result of the inability of the soft alluvial subsoil to withstand the pressure. Attempts to correct, or even halt, the lean (4m at the top) have so far proved unsuccessful, and the tower is closed to the public at present.

The **Baptistery** (Battistero), begun in 1153, was not finally completed until the Gothic dome was added in the 14C. Impressive and imposing from the outside, the interior is equally majestic – with a sense

The tower began to lean even before it was half built. Architects attempted to build the remainder at an angle, to correct the lean, but to no avail.

of light and spaciousness, beautiful marbles, **Nicola Pisano**'s fine pulpit, and many splendid panels, sculptures and statues.

The fourth 'must' set on the grassy expanse of the Piazza del Duomo is the **Cemetery** (Camposanto). This was the city's main cemetery in the 13C, reputed to contain soil brought back by Crusaders from the Holy Land for the burial of the rich and famous. The rectangular cloister still has some lovely frescoes by **Gozzoli**, **Gaddi**, and **Aretino**, though most were destroyed in World War II.

The **Botanical Gardens** (Orto Botanico) – a delightful green oasis in the heart of the city – are one of the oldest botanical gardens in Europe. From here, you can walk to the **Piazza dei Cavalieri**, with its church and neighbouring buildings by **Vasari**. Note also the complicated spires of the church of **St**

Mary of the Thorn (Santa Maria della Spina). The **Cathedral Museum** (Museo dell'Opera del Duomo), **Sinopia Museum** (Museo delle Sinopie) and the **National Museum** (Museo Nazionale di San Matteo) are all worth a visit.

Pistoia

A city with many fine 12C-14C buildings clustered around the **Piazza del Duomo**, notably the **Cathedral of San Zeno**, with its famous silver altar of St James, and the **Baptistery**, by tradition designed by **Pisano**. The frieze on the facade of the **del Ceppo Hospital** (Ospedale del Ceppo) is a parade of the work of **Giovanni della Robbia**.

Prato

The vast Germanic **Imperial Castle** (Castello dell'Imperatore), built for the Emperor Frederick II, cannot fail to impress. However, the churches, too, are equally memorable, notably **Santa Maria delle Carceri** and the duomo **Santo Stefano**, with its frescoes by **Filippo Lippi**, and exterior Pulpit of the Holy Girdle of Mary. It is appropriate that the holy relic should be an item of clothing – Prato is a major centre for wool and cloth, making textiles and knitwear in its unattractive suburbs.

The tiny church of St Mary of the Thorn nestles beside the broad span of the River Arno.

San Gimignano

Three rings of walls and 79 towers – this was the 'Town of the Fine Towers' at the height of its importance. Such defences were necessary until **Bishop Gimignano** finally repulsed the invaders and gave the town his name. The stone towers, rocketing above its two squares, have made the town famous: they were built by feuding 14C families.

EXPLORING TUSCANY

Although only 17 towers remain, they have
survived in San Gimignano better than
elsewhere in Italy only because it became
impoverished. It was once common for
towns to destroy such structures when they
were no longer of any use. They must have
been inconvenient residences and were
often joined at their tops by wooden bridges
and walkways. The country views from the
biggest, over the town hall, are spectacular,

and San Gimignano is an excellent base for some lovely country walks. The town itself can be viewed from the ruined **Rocca**. Today, one of the great treats of Tuscany is to go into the **Collegiate Church** (La Collegiata, often called the Duomo) and illuminate with a coin the bright frescoes which cover the walls of the nave – vivid and detailed pictures by **Bartolo di Fredi** (north aisle) and **Barna da Siena** (south aisle). There are also frescoes by **Ghirlandaio** in the Chapel of Santa Fina.

There are spectacular views of San Gimignano and the surrounding countryside from the top of one of the town's defensive towers.

Sansepolcro – north-east of Arezzo

This town, near the appropriately-named **Alps of the Moon**, was the home of one of Italy's famous 15C painters, **Piero della Francesca**. There are several important works in the **Municipal Museum** (Museo Civico). Look, in particular, for the famous *Resurrection* and the *Virgin Mary of Mercy*. The ochre-coloured **duomo** has a rose window, while inside there are glazed statues and an ornate arched tabernacle of **della Robbia**.

Siena

Siena is a legendary medieval town, enfolded in three hills, which retains much of its ancient allure. Its narrow Gothic streets, packed with palaces, dip up and down and are refreshingly cool, even on the hottest of days. Built in a Y-shape, Siena emerged in the Middle Ages to defeat the army of Florence in 1260. Later reversals in Siena's fortunes included lost battles and the dreadful visit of the Black Death in 1348, which completely halted the enlargement of the cathedral. You can see the intended extent by walls marked to the south.

A tour should take in the main attractions,

ending in the spectacular shell-shaped **Piazza del Campo**, where twice each year the **Palio** flutters brilliant banners as ten of the city's 17 districts compete in the famous horse race round the square. If you visit on 2 July or 16 August, you can see this, one of the most spectacular (and probably the most hazardous) of Tuscany's festivals.

Cafés cluster round the rim of this huge paved square and the harmonious arc of ruddy brick facades faces the triple-bayed arches of the graceful **Town Hall** (Palazzo Pubblico), with the narrow dart of the **Torre del Mangia** at one end. It can be climbed – if you have the energy, for it is 88m (290ft) high, but affords stunning views over Siena. The Palazzo Pubblico houses the **Museo Civico**, which largely consists of frescoes illustrating events in Italy's history. There is a fresco depicting the city's banking empire by **Lorenzetti**. An important cycle of frescoes by the same artist is in the **Peace Room** (Sala della Pace).

The **Cathedral** (Duomo di Sante Maria dell'Assunta) is fabulous in its effect and its ostentation. It has many opulent treasures, from its black and white marble facade to the exceptional interior; including the superb **Nicola Pisano** pulpit, the extraordinary 15C-16C sculpted, inlaid marble pavements (56 in all, the work of about 40 artists, portraying mythological figures and scenes from the Old Testament) and the polychrome busts of the popes around the upper part of the nave. In the Renaissance **Piccolomini Library** are **Pinturicchio**'s frescoes and statues. The adjoining **Cathedral Museum** (Museo dell'Opera del Duomo) houses statues from the cathedral by **Pisano** and **Duccio**'s famous

The magnificent entrance to Siena's Cathedral (Duomo di Santa Maria dell'Assunta), with its striking black and white marble stripes.

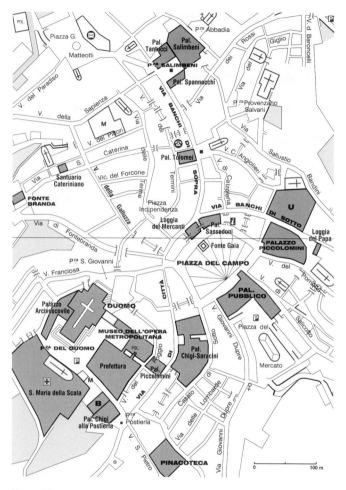

Map of Siena

Virgin in Majesty (Maestà). Oddly placed at the rear is a **Baptistery** (Battistero San Giovanni) with a font with gilded bronze panels by **Donatello**, **Ghiberti** and **della Quercia**. A range of 13C-16C Sienese works are housed in the **Picture Gallery** (Pinacoteca Nazionale).

There is much else to see in Siena, not least some splendid palaces situated off the **Via di Città** and **Via Banchi di Sopra**: Palazzo Piccolomini, Palazzo Chigi-Saracini, Palazzo Tolomei, and those around the **Piazza Salimbeni**.

Volterra

The ancient town of Volterra, set midway between Siena and the sea and positioned spectacularly on its windswept mountain top, may appear grim and austere, but it offers a garland of surprises once through the Etruscan gate, **Porta all'Arco**. One of the strongest cities of the Etruscan league, it was then called Velathri. In bleak surroundings, ringed with massive walls, the city must have been a stern and forbidding fortress.

The present-day Volterra only occupies about a third of the area of Velathri. The medieval town is based around the **Piazza dei Priori**. The **Palazzo dei Priori** is probably the oldest town hall in Tuscany. The 12C **Cathedral** has a fine ceiling and a **Gozzoli** fresco; the octagonal **Baptistery** has a font by **Sansovino.**

Two major museums are the **Picture Gallery** (Pinacoteca) and the important **Etruscan Museum** (Museo Etrusco Guarnacci), with more than 600 Etruscan funerary urns. There is a Roman theatre, and the rather sinister-looking 15C **Fortezza Medicea**, currently a prison.

EXPLORING TUSCANY

MOUNTAINS AND HILL TOWNS

Inland, the Tuscan geography changes. Hills do abut the sea, but once away from the coastal plain you come rapidly into hilly, even mountainous, areas. There are high peaks and isolated hills, as sudden butts of stone push up from valley floors and hillsides. Some are actually the remains, or plugs, of ancient volcanoes.

These made good defensive posts, since they allowed wide views of the surrounding country and were often solitary, their summits providing safe, if dramatic, perches for tight-knit towns. The higher the town, the better it could view and control the surrounding area, and the easier it was for it to defend itself against attack at a time when every town was at war with its neighbour.

There are many such hill towns in Tuscany, some, like **Montalcino**, are almost unchanged since medieval times. Once you have toiled up the steep approach roads you have a real sense of going back in time. Inside the medieval walls you find a tight net of streets, small squares and stepped passages, the tall houses adapted cleverly to the narrow, confined spaces.

The other upland area in Tuscany is the great backbone of Italy, the **Apennines**. This mountain chain runs along the eastern edge of Tuscany. Here the scenery is dramatic, as the narrow roads climb steeply up to high passes.

The mountains are favourite spots for winter sports and walking, hiking, climbing and skiing are popular. **Monte Falco** has ski runs, while ski lifts drape the slopes of **Mount Amiata**. From it you can see **Monte Cetona**, site of an important Bronze Age

The 16C walls and its hill top situation once protected the town of Colle di Val d'Elsa.

Built on rocky outcrops, the hill towns had excellent views over the surrounding valleys, affording warning of impending attacks.

settlement. Sadly, both mountains have been disfigured with gaunt crosses at their summits. From **Stia**, at the source of the Arno, there are walks up the neighbouring peaks of **Monte Falco** and **Monte Falterona**. A mountain in the sea is the near-circular **Monte Argentario**, which is wonderful for wild flowers in spring. You can walk or drive up to the radio mast at the top.

The steep-sided ravine scenery typical of the Apuan Alps.

BEACHES AND COASTAL TOWNS

Tuscany's coastline is little known outside Italy, but the curving coast is fringed with sandy beaches and resorts of all kinds. The northernmost section, some 60km stretching down as far as Livorno, is known as the **The Versilia**, or the **Tuscan Riviera**, which has the most commercially developed beach resorts. At the other extreme in the south are the marshy lagoons of the **Maremma**, with some finest beaches, such as **Marina di Alberese**.

The busy resort of Viareggio is well laid out, with a long sea-front backed by shops, restaurants and hotels.

The Versilia

The eight resorts along the Versilia have been developed along similar lines, with a marina complete with hotels, restaurants and cafés, and shops arranged in a grid of

streets next to the beaches. Some sections of the beach are free (marked *Spiaggia Pubblica*), while *stabilimenti* offer the use of beach huts and sun chairs in exchange for an entrance fee.

Viareggio is the biggest and best known resort. A large town with a huge beach set against pines and the soft outlines of hills, it is constantly busy, with plenty to do and modern facilities. **Forte dei Marmi** is an attractive resort with a sandy beach, backed by woods, named after its 18C fortress. **Marina di Carrara** is a port for marble as well as having a beach, while **Marina di Massa** is quiet and elegant, with a wide beach.

Other Beaches

There is plenty of choice among the other beaches, and you are sure to find your own personal favourite. The following is a selection to whet the appetite. **Castiglioncello,** an ancient town perched on a promontory, has an interesting museum. **Castiglione della Pescaia**, set in woods on the Maremma coast, with a Spanish castle and old walls, is the major beach of this region. **Marina di Cecina** nestles by a pine-clustered river mouth, while **Punta Ala** affords views of Elba and has good swimming. **Quercianella**, charmingly set in woods, contrasts with **San**

Fringed by trees, and with the mountains forming a backdrop, Forte dei Marmi is a most attractive beach.

Vincenzo, a very popular, large, lively and noisy resort. **Talamone**, situated on a rocky point by a national park, has views to Monte Argentario, which has its own beaches. **Tirrenia**, more exclusive than most, lies on a stretch of protected coast.

EXPLORING TUSCANY

THE ISLANDS

For those who like a back-to-nature holiday,
Tuscany's islands are ideal. Just off the
southern coast there is a cluster; some may
be little visited by tourists, others are not
easy to get to (ferries from the mainland or
Elba connect somewhat eratically). **Elba** is by
far the largest, offering lots of possibilities
for a complete holiday (*see* p.46). One that is
almost an island, being moored to the
mainland only with three
fragile strips of sand, is **Monte
Argentario** (*see* p. 83).

*Elba lives up to its
reputation of being
one of Italy's most
beautiful islands.*

Between Tuscany and
Corsica, the islands are all
small yet mountainous. They
offer the chance to discover
the island while walking and
hiking, with good swimming,
underwater exploration,
camping and simple meals.

Off Monte Argentario,
Giglio is the largest of these
islands, and can be reached by
car ferry. Giglio has tiny resorts
and underwater fishing to
offer. The Tyrrhenian Sea is
very rich in sealife; fish
restaurants abound. The island
also produces its own local
wine. To the south-east, tiny
Giannutri has a Roman villa.

Further out is the
uninhabited **Montecristo**. It is
now a nature park that can be
visited from Elba. Closer
inshore are **Pianosa** and
Capraia. The former is volcanic
with a lake, Il Laghero, in a

one-time crater. Capraia, 'island of goats', with its dramatic scenery and watchtowers (piracy was a problem in earlier times), and a castle at Capraia village, will appeal to those interested in rambling and wildlife. Parts of the island have difficult access, and its western side is still rough and hostile, but there is good underwater swimming in pellucid waters, windsurfing, boating and fishing. Like the equally isolated Pianosa, the island also served as a prison in the past.

TERME

For many visitors, Tuscany offers an attraction that is increasingly popular with the health conscious – visits to spa towns to take the waters and sample the variety of treatments offered, from mudbaths to massage. Tapping into the sulphurous heat sources just below the earth's surface, the mineral-rich water and warm springs are used for a range of treatments. What used to be known as 'taking the cure', now includes a variety of modern health services, both as therapy and as a form of relaxation.

Spas, or *terme* are often charmingly old-fashioned in appearance, and many are set in a scenic background of gardens and greenery. **Montecatini Terme** is probably the most popular and upmarket spa. Set in the lovely gardens at **Parco delle Terme**, there are nine thermal establishments, all with warm baths. Nearby is **Monsummano Terme**, with vapour baths. **Bagni di Lucca**, with its warm sulphur springs, is said to be the oldest terme still in use. It is reputed to have been used as early as the 11C by Countess Matilda, ruler of northern Tuscany, while more recent famous patrons include Shelley, Montaigne, Byron and Heine. **Chianciano Terme**, near Montepulciano, is a major spa, though more modern in design, with chalybeate and saline baths. **Bagni di Vignoni** and **Bagni San Filippo**, in the Orcia valley, both have hot sulphur springs, while **Casciano di Bagni**, near Cetona, offers hot mud baths.

Near the 12C terme at Bagni di Lucca, is the 12C Devil's Bridge.

HOLIDAYING WITH CHILDREN

The Italians adore children, and the Tuscans are no exception. Wherever you go, you will see children being paraded, admired and unashamedly spoiled. This warmth towards children means that you will not find a problem taking children into restaurants or bars – they will be welcomed.

The splendours of Tuscany's art, architecture, hill towns and cathedrals may not receive much applause from children, but Tuscany offers plenty of choice for families with children, so that everyone's needs can be catered for.

Beaches and coastline

The **Tuscan Riviera** offers excellent facilities for families, with wide, clean, safe beaches, with cafés, hotels, restaurants and beach shops in the marina area of the town. There are many other beaches to explore along the Tuscan coastline (*see* pp. 67-68).

Theme Parks

The **Pinocchio Theme Park** (Parco di Pinocchio) at Collodi, home town of **Carlo Lorenzini** who created Pinocchio, has a series of sculptures telling the story of Pinocchio. There are good picnic facilities and outdoor restaurants and adults will enjoy exploring the grounds, dotted with many sculptures.

In addition, many of the main towns and cities have parks and play areas, where the

Maremma Park has some of the best beaches, with white sand, fringed with trees.

Children taking a rest on the steps of a church.

children will mix happily with the locals. Despite the lack of a common language, they will soon be playing together.

Nature Parks

Maremma Park is the largest, and because of its size remains uncrowded and unspoilt. Children will enjoy watching the *butteri* (the local 'cowboys') herding the long-horned white cattle that graze the area. They re-enact their contest with Buffalo Bill Cody's men in spectacular shows put on in **Alberese** in August. Maremma is good for cycling and has some of the best beaches.

There are also nature parks at **Bolgheri**, **Orbetello** and **Monte Cetona**.

Festivals and Fairs

Children (and adults) will enjoy the colourful spectacle of the various festivals, staged by almost every Tuscan town at some point in the year. Check with the local tourist information office for details. **Siena's Palio** is the most famous, but there are plenty of others to choose from, ranging from a local carnival to a medieval-style joust. Whatever the scale, the enthusiasm of the participants, the wonderful costumes and the intense excitement of the events guarantee to entertain all ages (*see* p.91).

There are big **fairs** at Impruneta and Greve, with its puppet theatre, and **Pelago** has a lively buskers festival during July.

Other Attractions

Sant'Agata has a **Museum of Automata**. **Massa Marittima** has a **Mining Museum** (Museo della Miniera) set in an old mine. There are **zoos** at **Poppi** and **Verginina** (near Pistoia).

GAZETTEER

Abbadia San Salvatore
– west of Chiusi

A lively resort (mainly for winter sports) on **Monte Amiata**. Its ancient towered abbey church, once the richest in Tuscany, has an impressive set of sculpted columns.

Abetone – near Pistoia

A popular ski resort near the border with Emilia; in summer it is a centre for country walks and climbing in the lovely wooded hills.

Anghiari
– north-east of Arezzo

Anghiari is a very quiet town now, but two violent fights occurred here, the first one depicted by **Leonardo da Vinci** in a Florentine fresco (now destroyed) between the Florentines and the Milanese Visconti. This walled town, high above the Tiber, has an interesting local museum; coats-of-arms add colour to the civic palace.

Ansedonia – near Orbetello

Almost at the southernmost point of Tuscany, a fascinating Roman town (Cosa) has been excavated over the past 50 years. Digs have revealed a villa with mosaics, a forum, temples and a castle ringed with walls, with one gate surviving. There are fine views across Orbetello's lagoon from the old acropolis. Try the fish soup here.

Arcidosso
– near Abbadia San Salvatore

A holiday resort, this medieval town situated on the slopes of Monte Amiata has castle ruins. Nearby is an 11C church.

Artimino – west of Florence

Originally an Etruscan town, some of the stones from Etruscan tombs were used to build **San Leonardo**, a Romanesque church. Just above this walled village a large outdoor stairway marks the 16C **Villa Ferdinanda** (noted for its fine fireplaces). A distinctive local wine is made here.

Asciano – south-east of Siena

Two museums are found in this small walled town; a collection of Sienese pictures are in the **Arte Sacra Museum**, while the redundant church of **San Bernardino** has Etruscan finds from a nearby necropolis.

Barga – near Lucca

This beautiful and fashionable town boasts vast, yet satisfyingly simple, wood-ceilinged **duomo**, with a beautiful pulpit (13C) and other fine Romanesque sculptures.

Bibbiena – near Arezzo
This one-time Etruscan town sits under the mountains north of Arezzo, in the Arno valley. The **Casentino countryside** is popular with Italian holiday-makers and is rightly renowned for its beauty. Local **salami** is worth sampling.

Bivigliano – north of Florence
A resort with fine views and, at **Monte Senario**, the mother house of the **Servite Order**, founded in the 13C.

Borgo San Lorenzo
– north of Florence
Now largely modernised (though its church has a Romanesque campanile), this is a good centre for discovering the villages of the seductive **Mugello**, also known as the Sieve Valley (Val di Sieve).

Buonconvento
– south of Siena
Distinguished by its three tall gates and commanding walls, this pretty town of ancient alleys has a museum of Tuscan works.

Calci – east of Pisa
Woods of pine and chestnut surround the town of Calci and its fine arcaded Romanesque church, built in the local style. The campanile remains unfinished: inside, Roman columns

Castellina in Chianti's unusual 15C covered walkway was built as a defence.

support the roof. Not far off, is **Charterhouse** (Certosa di Pisa), founded in the 14C but with ecclesiastical buildings of various dates.

Campaldino – near Bibbiena
Arezzo went to war against the Florentines here, the latter winning. The battle site is marked with a column.

Capalbio – near Orbetello
This walled town, founded by Rome, is within the Maremma Park: town restaurants present an array of wild boar, gamebirds and deer, in season. 10 km away is the vast necropolis of **Marsiliana**.

Caprese Michelangelo
– north of Arezzo
The **Casa del Podestà**, by the castle, is where sculptor, poet and painter **Michelangelo** was born; he was baptised in the church. The ground floor museum has copies of the artist's work.

Castellina in Chianti
– east of Poggibonsi
The ancient fortified castle is the seat of the Chianti Producers' Organization and the village is typical of this wine-producing region. It has imposing Etruscan remains, notably **Monte Calvario**, a huge

tumulus tomb with burial chambers.

Castelnuovo Val di Cecina
– near Volterra
A small town, surrounded by woods, solitary, yet with several fine medieval buildings and wide views. Nearby **Montecatini Val di Cecina**, contains the castle of the Volterra bishops and has **della Robbia** terracottas in the Romanesque parish church.

Castiglioncello
– south of Livorno
A favoured seaside resort situated on a pine-tree clad point, Castiglioncello has Etruscan origins (with a museum). It gained its prominent watchtower from Florence, as a defence against piracy.

Castiglion Fiorentino
– south of Arezzo
A medieval circular wall encompasses Castiglion Fiorentino, and the handsome high-spired church marks this town, with coats-of-arms decorating its main square. There is also an art gallery and a castle.

Castiglione della Pescaia
– near Grosseto
A 14C castle clings to the high rock above the harbour. Long

The courtyard of the Governor's Palace in Certaldo.

sandy beaches and pinewoods contribute to this resort's charm. Inland is **Vetulonia**, an Etruscan site rich in gold, first excavated 100 years ago, with 7C BC tombs.

Castiglione d'Orcia
– south-west of Pienza

There is a whole group of towns of the 'd'Orcia'. This one is a hill town with well preserved walls. **Rocca d'Orcia** is a pretty old village, shadowed by a ruined tower.

Castello
– north-west of Florence

Here you will find several Medici villas. One, the **Villa di Castello**, has a famous 16C garden which may be visited.

Castello di Brolio
– near Poggibonsi

Noted for its vast 9C castle,

restored by the **Ricasoli family** 1000 years later. You can actually stay in this brooding castle, with its terraced gardens and stern brick towers, set in a huge estate.

Cecina – south of Livorno

Once a Roman posting stop on the **Via Aurelia**, the town was reclaimed from the marshes in the 19C. **Marina di Cecina** is its resort, with long sandy beaches, set at the edge of pine forests.

Certaldo
– south-west of Florence

This romantic, red-brick town, set on a low hill, was **Boccaccio**'s home. He retired and died here, in a house now rebuilt and housing a museum. Noted for its wines, the lower part of the town sprawls by the River Elsa which runs along the wooded valley.

Certosa del Galluzzo
– south of Florence

The 14C **Carthusian monastery**, which peers from its hill, contains three great cloisters and many treasures, including **della Robbias** and **Pontormo frescoes**. It is now a Cistercian house, where the monks make and sell a liqueur.

Cetona – south-west of Chiusi

There are not only Etruscan hoards here, in the **Palazzo Terrosi**, but also traces of pre-historic man in a series of caves. Nearby, is a **Franciscan monastery** with ancient frescoes.

Colle di Val d'Elsa
– near San Gimignano

Enter this town of **glass-makers**, and **palaces** through the upper **Porta Nuova,** set in medieval walls. It is on two levels, the Colle Bassa and the Colle Alta, and has wonderful views. In the upper town is a 17C **duomo** and **Santa Maria**, a simple Romanesque church.

Collodi – west of Lucca

Carlo Lorenzini, Pinocchio's creator, took the name of his town as his pseudonym, Carlo Collodi. Scenes of the life of the famous puppet are outlined in the **Pinocchio Theme Park** (Parco di Pinocchio). There is also the 17C **Villa Garzoni** to see, with lovely fountains in its terraced water gardens. Collodi is also known for its *torta*, or local cake.

Comeana – west of Florence

Early **Etruscan tombs**, one monumental, cluster near this town.

Empoli – west of Florence

The **Cathedral**, Sant'Andrea, is basically Romanesque though earlier in origin. It has a striking marble facade, built in imitation of San Miniato in Florence. The local industry is glass-blowing. It has an interesting museum in the **Collegiata**.

Gaiole – north of Siena

A renowned Chianti wine centre, with a 14C church.

Gargonza – west of Siena

In exile from Florence, **Dante** lived in this walled village.

Greve – south of Florence

This pretty town, important for producing Chianti Classico, has an unusual arcaded square, **Piazza Matteotti**, of irregular design and surrounded by buildings with colonnades shading many small shops. There is a splendid monument to the 16C explorer of North America's coastline, **Giovanni da Verazzano**. The wine festival, held every September, is a lively event.

Impruneta
– south of Florence
Beside wine, this town has always specialized in terracotta. Here you can find the typical earthenware, from tiles to statues, both on buildings and as articles for sale. Straw hats are also made here, and there is a horse fair in the arcaded piazza each October.

La Verna – near Bibbiena
Here, at this spacious church situated on a rock overlooking the **Casentino country**, **St Francis** received the stigmata in 1224, and it has become a place of pilgrimage. He also founded

There are extensive views reaching to the sea from Massa Marittima.

the monastery, now basically a cluster of buildings in later styles.

Magliano in Toscana
– north-east of Orbetello

This walled town on the **Via Aurelia** was originally Etruscan (there is a burial site to the south), and has 16C gates. There are two churches worth visiting – **San Martino** (Romanesque) and **San Giovanni Battista** (Gothic-Romanesque).

Massa – near Carrara

Set between the Apuan Alps and the sea, Massa has a castle, a delightful ducal palace (17C **Palazzo Cibo Malaspina**) and a beach at **Marina di Massa**, protected by the hills behind. Local dishes include wonderful concoctions of fresh, green vegetables.

Massa Marittima
– north of Grosseto

This was once the most important centre in the **Maremma**, owing to mines excavated by the Etruscans and Romans for silver, copper and iron. The **Mining Museum** (Museo della Miniera) is worth a visit. The town is built on two levels, unusually the Gothic **Città Nuova** is the upper one, while the lower **Città Vecchia** is

Romanesque, and contains a splendid Cathedral, with a fine campanile. Like the solid, turreted palazzo comunale, it contains many treasures.

Meleto – near Poggibonsi

A delightful 11C castle survives (though it is not open to the public). Nearby is the wine-producing village of **Radda in Chianti**, which also has a castle.

Montalcino – south of Siena

A walled hill town, this was once a pawn between Florence and Siena, who destroyed it in 1260. It has a formidable castle and several museums, but it is most famous for a fabled wine, **Brunello di Montalcino**. Nearby is a superb example of 12C building. The **Abbey of Sant'Antimo** is a golden presence in a wide valley, stately outside, luminous with alabaster carvings inside. If you only have time to see one country church, make it this one.

Monte Argentario
– south of Grosseto

Although connected to the mainland by road from Orbetello and Ansedonia, this remains essentially an island, dominated by a 655m (2 150ft) peak. An encircling shore road links the popular beach resorts

The lovely church of Sant'Antimo nestles by the hillside near Montalcino.

of **Port'Ercole** and **Porto Santo Stefano**, which provide boats and ferries to nearby islands. Try the fish dishes, such as *fritto misto di mare* and the Tuscan spiced fish stew, *cacciucco*.

Monte Oliveto Maggiore
– near Siena
The Tuscan-red abbey buildings cluster grandly in a park with a cloistered church, fish ponds and pleasant gardens. Founded in 1319, this is the mother house of the **Olivetan order**.

Monte Amiata
– near Abbadia San Salvatore
A one-time volcano (with mineral deposits, including mercury, still mined here), the mountain is now a ski centre, with the highest peak in the area.

Monterchi – east of Arezzo
This part-walled town has a rarity – although difficult to get to see – one of **della Francesca**'s madonnas is in a former school on Via Reglia.

Monteriggioni
– north-east of Siena
From this tiny fortified hill town, still surrounded by 14 towers, the Sienese watched for the Florentines. Very quiet now (only 20 or so families inhabit the silent streets), it is atmospheric and has fine views and good restaurants.

Monte San Savino
– south-west of Arezzo
The major artists **Sansovino** (born here) and **Sangallo the Elder** collaborated on several buildings in this majolica-making town.

Montevarchi – west of Arezzo
Shadowed by a castle, this ancient but much-altered town offers the handsome arcaded **San Lorenzo**, gold and sculptures by the **della Robbias** and Arno fossils at the **Accademia**.

Monticchiello – near Pienza
A pretty walled hill town, with a rose window in its church. In summer, a theatre festival is presented here.

Orbetello – south of Grosseto
The town clusters along the central strip of land crossing fish-filled lagoons to Monte Argentario. There are Etruscan and 16C Spanish walls with gates, and a **baroque duomo**, with a fine original Gothic facade. There is also good seafood here, the speciality being eels.

Pescia – north-east of Lucca
A large commercial daily flower market is held here (open to the public to but flowers from 9am-noon). The town also holds a famous biennial flower show. There is architecture of several periods in this riverside town. Try the local asparagus and beans, and also an unusual stew, *cioncia*.

Piancastagnaio
– near Abbadia San Salvatore
Brooding square towers accent the **Rocca**, now a weapons museum.

Pienza
A long hill town, its narrow alleys are packed round a small piazza with a church, apparently in constant danger of slipping down the hill. **Palazzo Piccolomini**, with its dramatic hanging gardens, was the home of Pius II, who totally redesigned his birthplace in the 15C in an attempt to create an 'ideal town'. There are panoramic views over the Orcia valley from walks around the town.

Pietrasanta
– north of Viareggio
Stonework is practised here – onyx and marble. It is a place for sculptors to meet and work. The **duomo**, of several periods, has marble furnishings and sculpture. There is also a ruined fort.

Pitigliano – near Grosseto
Looking as if it has grown from

Monte Argentario is linked to the mainland by three thin strips of land.

the earth on its rock spur, the settlement was Etruscan, later ruled by Rome. The campanile was once part of its castle. The **Orsini Palace** (14C) has a fine courtyard and there is the oldest Italian synagogue. Cliff-tombs in lower walls are Etruscan.

Poggibonsi

This straggle of a town on Val d'Elsa is not especially attractive in itself, but it does provide the visitor with a good base for touring and for tasting Chianti. The town was badly damaged in World War II but has re-estab-lished itself as a wine and furniture centre. It is shadowed by an unfinished fort.

Poggio a Caiano
– west of Florence

The wide brick arches of the 15C villa here must have provided cool arcades for Medici nobles. **Sangallo** built this country house, which has lively frescoes, including a famous **Pontormo**.

Pontassieve – east of Florence

Surrounded by vineyards, this wine centre has a lively fair each May.

Pontremoli
– north of La Spezia
This tongue of Tuscany, all woods and hills, forms a spur in the region to the north-west, the valley of the Magra. Because of its vital stragegic position, the town was fought over by Florence and Genoa. It has an interesting **Archaeological Museum** in its high-perched castle. The range of architecture takes in a **baroque duomo**, a **rococo church** and an earlier one with a **Romanesque campanile**.

Popiglio – near Pistoia
A panoramic view down towards this settlement, with its ancient church and bridge, can be gained from the nearby village of **Piteglio**.

Poppi – north of Arezzo
A hill top town of the Casentino, Poppi presides over a wide stretch of the Arno laced with vines. There is a tall-towered **castello**, and ancient **town hall**, arcades along Via Cavour. **Mino da Fiesole** was born here: a picture of his is at Camaldoli.

Populonia – near Piombino
Iron ore from nearby Elba made the Etruscans powerful, and it was smelted here at their port. Above the sea, on a point, there are the remains of walls, remarkable Etruscan tombs, a

The peaceful and pretty square in the tiny hill town of Monteriggioni.

necropolis below, and a museum. The heavy-browed and crenellated towers of the upper town are 14C Pisan.

Pratolino – north of Florence
Once renowned for its magnificent garden, Pratolino has now lost all of its original plan, except for a huge statue by **Giambologna**.

Radicofani – south of Chiusi
Here on basalt rock, **Hadrian IV**, sole English pope, built a castle.

Roselle Scavi
– north-east of Grosseto
This deserted town has extensive **Etruscan** walls and gates, as well as **Roman** remains – an amphitheatre, houses and a forum.

San Giovanni Valdarno
– west of Arezzo
The great painter, **Masaccio**, was born here. In **Piazza Masaccio** an airily arcaded church, **San Lorenzo**, contains his early frescoes, with a picture gallery and **della Robbia** terracotta works.

San Miniato – east of Pisa
Standing over the Arno, the ancient castle has two towers, one a campanile. The **cathedral** is still visibly Romanesque. The museum of church art reflects a town of churches, with many treasures, including a **Donatello** tomb. There is a mystery play cycle in August.

San Quirico d'Orcia
This walled town possesses a fine church with columned and sculpted 12C doorways.

San Romano
– west of San Miniato
San Romano is best known for its battle between Florence and Siena, recorded in three paintings by **Uccello**. Once displayed together, the separate paintings are now in the Uffizi Gallery (Florence), the Louvre (Paris) and the National Gallery (London).

Sant'Andrea in Percusina
– south of Florence
Visit **Machiavelli**'s house, where he wrote his famous works, has now become a hotel and restaurant.

San Vincenzo
– south-west of Volterra
A lively, not to say crowded, resort with many attractions and nightlife for holidaymakers, particularly the young. Its wide sandy **beach** looks toward Elba. There is a **Roman** tower, and nearby are **Etruscan remains**. Try local seafood

dishes served with rice, such as cuttlefish, as well as the better-known *fritto misto*.

Sarteano – near Chiusi

With **Etruscan origins**, Sarteano has **mineral pools**, a 15C **castle** and a palazzo.

Scarperia – north of Florence

Scarperia is a town of the Mugello, making wrought iron and cutlery. A fine **palazzo pretorio** of 1306 simulates Palazzo Vecchio of Florence. It is worth a detour, to see **Bosco ai Frati**, a charming 15C

A golden summer landscape, looking across the Orcia Valley to Pienza.

convent, with a crucifix by the great **Donatello**.

Sesto Fiorentino – near Prato
The Ginori family introduced **porcelain** in the 18C and the Doccia factory operates a **Porcelain Museum**.

Settignano – east of Florence
Almost a suburb of Florence, yet still keeping its separateness, the town is famous for being the birthplace of several artists. **Michelangelo** grew up here and the actress **Eleonora Duse** stayed with **d'Annuzio**. The a;rt critic **Bernard Berenson** lived here; his Villa Tatti is now owned by Harvard University. Nearby, is the **Villa Gamberaia**; this handsome 16C building has original parterre gardens.

Sorano – near Sovana
This consists of a tight cluster of tall buildings with a 15C **castle**, poised on a rock, with many **Etruscan** tombs cut into the rock and cliff face.

Sovana – north of Pitigliano
An isolated settlement, Sovana was rather run down but has now been much restored. It was a town of some importance until the 13C, as is indicated by a ruined castle, the palaces and a part Gothic, part Romanesque cathedral, with fine reliefs. **Santa Maria** has a marble ciborium, unique in Tuscany. Nearby is ancient **Saturnia**. There are also **Etruscan** cemeteries.

Staggia – south of Poggibonsi
This medieval mountain village has a three-towered castle.

Stia – north of Arezzo
This upper Arno town has a 12C church, with its own **della Robbia**.

Torre del Lago Puccini – near Viareggio
Puccini's lakeside villa can be visited. All his operas save *Turandot* were conceived here. Although a creative man, he loved hunting: guns are displayed alongside the opera souvenirs. He is buried in the chapel, with his wife. His operas are performed here in summer.

Vallombrosa – west of Florence
This old-style resort is famed for its splendid monastery. It has, along with nearby **Saltino**, restaurants and wooded walks.

Vespignano – near Borgo San Lorenzo
Giotto, whose realistic style revolutionized art, was born here.

Vetulonia – north of Grosseto
This rich maritime city was important to the **Etruscans**, with ruins and a very early necropolis nearby. The site of a Roman victory in 224 BC, it gave Rome the symbols of toga and fasces.

Vicchio – south-east of Borgo San Lorenzo

There is a small art museum, but Vicchio is better known as the birthplace of **Fra Angelico** and home of sculptor **Benvenuto Cellini**.

Vicopisano – east of Pisa
On a hill beneath **Monte Pisano**, it has a fortress with towers restored by **Brunelleschi** and an 11C Romanesque church.

Villa Medici – near Fiesole
Michelangelo's 15C country palace, with its views towards Florence, is acclaimed for setting the Renaissance style.

Vinci – north of Empoli
At Vinci, there are examples of **Leonardo da Vinci**'s inventions and drawings. He was born at **Anchiano**, nearby. As well as the **Museo Vinciano**, visit the **Guidi Castle**.

ENJOYING YOUR VISIT

Weather

Tuscany has a typical continental climate, with hot and sometimes uncomfortably humid summers, and cool yet not generally too cold winters. There is a fairly low level of precipitation and in summer you are sure of extended dry days.

In winter, this can affect the skiing, but as a rule enough snow accumulates on the mountains and up high there is brilliant winter sunshine (not always true of the lower-lying towns). Temperatures can, however, change dramatically in winter as you go inland, with very cold days in the upper valleys and mountains.

In summer, the reverse is the case, with hotter and less agreeable temperatures as you get further inland. It is usually cooler at higher altitudes, but the lower areas, valley floors and the cities can be uncomfortably hot and sticky. Near the coast, there is often a cooling breeze, especially in the evenings.

Spring and autumn provide the best weather for most visits, and for driving and town visits this is an ideal time.

Calendar of Events

Most special festivals and re-creations of historic pastimes and events occur in summer, though some are in early spring. Check with the Italian Tourist Board on specific dates and times before you go. Many towns have local markets, which can be augmented with secondhand bargain stalls and flea markets. There are commercial horse and cattle, wine and produce fairs, which are interesting to watch. Look for announcements in the local press or on notice boards. Grape-gathering is a time for celebrations, after the grapes are all safely in. You may also come across travelling fairs and circuses, on age-old perambulations.

Here are some of the main events which are held annually:

Arezzo There is a choral festival in late August. In a lively medieval joust, knights from the city's four quarters attack a shield in the Joust of the Saracen (late August and September). On the first weekend of each month, there is an antiques fair in the Piazza Grande.

Bibbiena A carnival, with a Bello Ballo dance, is held in spring.

Barga This northern valley town has an opera festival in July.

Cortona There is a major, month-long antiques fair, from the end of August.

Impruneta A mule, horse and wine sale, the Fiera di San Luca, is held in October.

Fiesole Opera and summer performances take place in the Roman amphitheatre, with a festival of music, drama and film in June and July.

Florence Numerous events (antique, fashion, commercial fairs, art exhibitions, food and speciality markets) are held throughout the year. The Calcio is a football game in 16C costume, followed by fireworks (24 June). In the Explosion of the Cart (Scoppio del Carro) fireworks on a cart light up the Piazza del Duomo, commemorating the First Crusade (Easter Sunday). The Festa della Rificolona involves folklore and musical events (7 September). The May Music Festival (Maggio Musicale) includes concerts, ballet and opera (May-July).

Lari The cherry festival is held in May, followed by the peaches festival in August.

The medieval football at the Calcio, Florence, is always a colourful and energetic event.

Lucca Puccini and Boccherini's home town honours them with a music festival lasting most of the summer, using ancient churches. There is a separate festival at nearby Villa Reale. The Luminara di Santa Croce is a torchlight procession in which the Volto Santo (Holy Visage – a miraculous crucifix) is carried though the town (13 September). An antiques fair is held on the third weekend of each month.

Massa Marittima Held on the third Sunday in May and the second Sunday in August, Il Girifalco is a crossbow contest in medieval costume, with displays and shooting at mechanical birds.

Montepulciano This town must have more

special events for its size than anywhere else in Italy. Of note are the country fair in May and contemporary art shows at the end of September/early October. The Cantiere Internazionale d'Arte combines 20C music and opera, performed in the Teatro Poliziano (first two weeks of August). The Bruscello is a costumed re-creation of the town's history, held in mid-August. On the last Sunday of the same month, the 14C Bravìo delle Botti is held, a parade when men of the town's eight districts race with barrels (a good wine is made here). Afterwards there is a big celebratory dinner around the Piazza.

Monticchiello There is a summer theatre festival held in July.

Pelago In this Mugello town, 'On the Road' – a celebration of busking, with assorted street entertainers – is held each July.

Piancastagnaio A November Fair is held for the chestnut harvest.

Pisa On 16 and 17 June the Luminara di San Ranieri involves candlelit parades and the Arno and quays are illuminated at night. The costumed Game of the Bridge (Gioco del Ponte), is on the last Sunday in June.

Pistoia A medieval joust, the Joust of the Bear (Giostra dell'Orso) is held on 25 July. Riders from each quarter of the city try to spear targets in the form of bears, while on horseback.

Pietrasanta Every summer for two months sculptors and craft workers display new works, mostly of marble.

Prato A pageant takes place on 8 September and on the same month, the Prato Fair. The Exposition of the Virgin's Girdle takes place on 1 May, 15 August and 8 September, and at Christmas.

The famous horse race in Siena, the Palio, is held twice a year.

Pontassieve This wine centre has a Chianti fair each May.

San Miniato A cycle of mystery plays is held each summer in late August.

Sansepolcro The balestra is a form of crossbow, and on the second Sunday of September in the Palio della Balestra, costumed citizens display the use of this lethal weapon as they battle with a rival town, Gubbio. There are also flag throwing displays. There is a local handicrafts and food fair in August. Also a Lenten fair.

Siena The Palio – twice a year (2 July, 16 August) this horse race between contestants from 10 of the 17 districts is run three times round the campo. Expensive, but very festive, very crowded, and worth trying to see. In August, there is a music festival. There are saints' day celebrations in March, November and December.

Torre del Lago Puccini An annual

celebration of the operas of Puccini is held at this lakeside country villa in August.

Torrita di Siena The local Palio dei Somari is held on the third Sunday in March. There is a mule race and flag juggling.

Viareggio A mammoth, pre-Lenten carnival held annually to lure out-of-season visitors to this large, popular seaside resort. It lasts for nearly three weeks in February, with a parade of floats every Sunday.

Food and Drink

This is one of the best parts of the world for good, plain food and drink. You can eat extremely well wherever you go. The food is simple, yet delicious and diverse, whether

There are plenty of good local wines to choose from.

you try formal eating or picnics using local produce, salamis, ham, or fresh vegetables.

Seafood, especially near Livorno, noted for its fish stew *cacciucco livornese*, is of all sorts, from eels to *fritto misto*, in which small fish are breaded and deep fried. Try more unusual offerings, such as salt cod in a thick sauce, fish stews and cuttlefish. Inland, there is plenty of fresh fish to choose from, but fish is never cheap here.

Tuscan food caters for all palates, from thick, filling soups (try the *ribollita*), often fortified with bread, to plainly-dressed pastas and rice dishes; from cold seafood to unusual salads; from grilled chicken to wild boar; from local hams to tripe. *Bue*, for

Tuscany is renowned for its excellent food and drink.

which the region is renowned, is fine beef
from the Val di Chiana. Here, local white
cattle provide meat that is famous
throughout Italy. For a treat, try *Bistecca alla
Fiorentina*, a thick, T-bone steak grilled over
either charcoal or vine shoots.

Remember that **pasta**, appealing though it
is in its many manifestations, is often a first
dish here, so don't overfill! Try it stuffed
with ricotta or in a hare sauce. Equally filling
can be *bruschetta* – toasted bread brushed
generously with garlic and olive oil. Starters
can be very imaginative, such as fried
marrow flowers or a salad of ricotta cheese,
avocado and tomato (the *tricolore*). White
beans, capers, cabbage, potatoes and
tomatoes are often used, frequently as the
base of a sauce. You can also find dishes
from other provinces to sample, such as
Emilia's famous **Parmesan cheeses** and
hams, or Naples' **pizzas**.

Sweets are not much eaten, though
chestnuts, grapes and eggs are used for

*The locally-
produced fruit and
vegetables are
excellent for self-
catering or picnics.*

desserts. Siena is noted for its *panforte* – a rich cake made from almonds, candied fruit and honey. The **ice cream** is excellent – a **gelateria** will have locally-made ones.

The area has noted local produce. Most famous is the golden-green **olive oil**, best from around Lucca. It enriches dishes and is good for the system, too. Top quality vegetables and fruits are grown. Wild mushrooms, notably **porcini**, are excellent in season. The few cheeses include **pecorino** and **ricotta**.

Allow lots of time when eating. It is a national pastime, and can take hours, much enjoyed indoors or out. Sitting on a warm evening over a lovely meal in a piazza, watching the world go by, while bells from clock towers spangle the brilliant summer air – these are the memories you will keep for years.

Wine, spirits and grappas

Tuscany has its own distinctive wines, which in this rich land are much prized. Red, white and rosé are augmented with fortified wines – Elba's **Aleatico** is a sweet wine. The sugary grapes of late autumn make rich dessert wines.

You are, of course, in the home of **Chianti**, and it is easy to follow a well-marked route that dips and dives up and down the grape-draped fields of the area. Winding north from east of Siena to Florence – this is the Chianti Route – well recommended both for tastings at numerous vineyards, and for the bosky, rural and charming views. You will see many signs featuring either a black cockerel or a rotund cupid. The **Gallo Nero** and the **Putto** are trademarks for the best of this wine.

Look out for the Chianti Classico sign.

The really busy time, when visits may not
be welcomed, is during the autumn grape-
gathering and pressing time, when resources
can be stretched. Many of the vineyards
offer free entry and the opportunity to buy.
Just make sure you have an extra driver, and
allow lots of time – Tuscan people are not to
be hurried when an important matter such
as wine is being considered.

Other red wines of the area come from a
wide scattering of localities, and it is true to
say you can hardly go anywhere in Tuscany
without seeing vines. Around Lucca the
product is red, in Pitigliano, Bolgheri and
Val d'Arbia wines are white. Top-ranking

wines such as **Brunello di Montalcino** are
well worth trying, or at San Gimignano try
the famed white **Vernaccia**. However, these
will not be cheap! Be daring and taste the
local products of small villages. Notable are
those of Artimino and Carmignano. Simpler
local ones may be earthy, plain or full
bodied, and have not travelled far beyond
their home, yet many are delicious.

Other drinks

*There is plenty of
opportunity to
sample the wines
before buying.*

You can get good beers at supermarkets and
shops, and bottled waters, both without and
con gas. Fruit cordials and juices are legion,
too. There are many drinks to be taken as
digestives after a meal, from a variety of
grappas to **liqueurs**, often made at
monasteries. In Chianti country you can eat
outside and then try a variety of these sweet
and sticky liqueurs – steeped in local herbs,
which are imprisoned in graceful glass
bottles. They add an exotic touch to the end
of a fine repast.

Shopping

For those for whom shopping is a major
reason for visiting a city or country, Tuscany
is a veritable treasure house. There is a
range of sophisticated products in the stores
and boutiques, some wonderfully old-
fashioned, exuding the atmosphere of
another age.

Italy excels in the production of fine
clothing in **leather**, **silk** and **wool**. Look for
men's and women's **shoes**, for all moods and
weathers. All sorts of articles, from model
dresses to children's shoes and the trendiest
trainers, reflect the latest in fashion. The
designs are among the best in the world in
all fields.

In addition, marvels are created in **jewellery** and silver, bronze and gold are used for **sculpture** and **reproductions**. These reflect classic tastes as well as introducing spectacular new ideas and materials. To see examples of new, innovative design, you need only saunter past chic shops, where some of the most spectacular designs in the world are cunningly presented. Boutiques and galleries, often in back streets, can offer one-off original creations you can be sure you will not see anywhere else when you get your treasure home.

Tuscany is well known for the high quality of its leather goods and shoes.

Antiques tend to be costly, but there are a few junk shops where you can search for bargains. Cities have specialist areas for pictures, antiques, rare books and prints.

When shopping, look for **alabaster** in Volterra, **terracotta** and **tiles** in Impruneta (where you also find **straw hats**), and typical **majolica ware** in Monte San Savino. Pietrasanta has **onyx** and **marble**, and Sesto Fiorentino fine **porcelain**. For **glass** look at Colle di Val d'Elsa, while **wrought iron** and **cutlery** can be found at Scarperia. Local **foodstuffs** are on sale everywhere, but check what you can take back. You are usually safe with dried, tinned or bottled goods. In chemists, look for **soaps**, **perfumes** and **oils**, as well as smart **sunglasses** and **cameras**.

While specialist shops can be excellent, you should not overlook department stores –

There are plenty of pavement cafés to refresh you while shopping.

even chain stores such as **Upim** – for cut-price clothes, toys, china and household goods. Dinnerware, glass and cutlery are often elegant and beautifully designed.

Florence takes on a new life at night, with entertainment to suit all tastes.

Entertainment and Nightlife

Much time is spent parading, café table-hopping and, particularly in warm weather, simply enjoying being sociable in town centres. Like all Italians, Tuscans love to promenade and show themselves off. The daily **passeggiata** is an institution often extending late into the evenings in summer.

Young and old enjoy sitting out in the lovely old piazzas in warm weather, gossiping on terraces over endless coffees and drinks. In the evening, families and couples join in. Everyone seems to know everyone else and drinks in the piazza can lead to supper 'al fresco', in the open; a wonderful pleasure.

Bigger towns have **cinemas**, still popular here. People often go in groups and avidly discuss the films afterwards. Most towns have **theatres**, where touring opera, dance and drama can be seen. Audiences enthusiastically participate; this is where opera was born! **Discos** and **pop events** are much enjoyed by the trendy, fashionable young; larger towns will often have two or three discos over a weekend, continuing till very late. Look out for posters announcing events, or at night just watch to see where the crowd is heading. In bigger coastal resorts, there is much night-time activity, not just in summer, and people will drive from nearby towns to attend pop and musical events.

In Florence, there are sophisticated **nightclubs** and **supper clubs** at the hotels, but they can be expensive. Also popular are

enoteca, which are wine bars where you can often buy local wines.

Ask for local giveaway magazines listing events, or the tourist information office (or even the hotel concierge!) can tell you what's on. Spa towns have become more modernized, with a variety of nightlife in the bigger ones to attract a young clientele, yet these old-fashioned towns are probably one of the few places where older people can pursue the more sedate social pleasures.

Sports

Team sports are popular and much followed. Like the rest of Italy, many locals are fans of **football** (or **calcio**). It is a principal spectator sport, with home teams being supported with great enthusiasm. The game is usually played on Sunday afternoons, times depending on the season. You will also see many local scratch teams kicking the ball around in parks.

Wintersports such as **skiing**, both downhill and cross country, **skating**, **tobogganing** and **solo sledding** are not as expensive as in some other European countries. They are very popular and are increasingly taken up by young people. For the ski enthusiast, the prime places are in the Apennines, or at Monte Amiata, which has many lifts.

Like most other countries, Italy has opened up a range of **sports centres** over the past decade. Even quite small towns may have facilities for indoor games, to exercise, lift weights, swim or slim. And hotels, particularly those catering for business people, will have spas where there are beauty salons, jacuzzis and whirlpools, saunas and massage services, and exercise machines. Jogging is not as popular in Italy as in some other countries, but **cycling** is followed with passion. There are cycle meets and races, and local **motor cycle** and track events.

Tennis is popular, on both grass and hard courts, and **golf** is a growing sport with new courses coming along. Check with the local tourist information office at your resort.

For specialist pursuits such as **walking**, **bird** or **wildlife watching**, try the Mugello, the Chianti country and the Maremma. There is more challenging walking, hiking, scrambling and climbing in the Apennines. The hilly country of the Garfagnana and the Maremma are ideal for **horse-riding**.

Fishing is a popular sport, both inland and on shore. If you want to fish, remember for freshwater angling you need a licence, but not for sea fishing.

Horse-riding is an excellent way to explore Tuscany's countryside.

THE BASICS

Before You Go

Visitors entering Italy should have a full passport valid to cover the period in which they will be travelling. No visa is required for members of EU countries or citizens of Eire, the United States, Canada, Australia and New Zealand. No vaccinations are necessary.

Getting There

Two airports serve the region of Tuscany: Pisa airport which receives most of the international traffic, and Florence airport where charter flights and domestic and a few international airlines land. Long-haul flights tend to arrive at Rome or Milan, from where flights connect with Pisa and Florence.

Charter flights and package tours to Florence and other towns in Tuscany are plentiful, both from Europe and North America, and there are many deals including car hire.

Trains from all over Italy, as well as from Paris and Zurich, arrive at the main railway stations in Florence and Pisa, via Turin and Genoa. Express trains run from London to Florence and Pisa. Services are fast and reliable, and there are many train passes and cards which offer reductions .

A relatively cheap way of travelling to Tuscany is by coach, and there are various services operating from Victoria, London and other major European cities.

Driving to Tuscany can be an enjoyable exercise if you have the time; routes from the east are now limited by disruption in former Yugoslavia, but there are many entry points from the north and north-west:

From France: via the Riviera through Genoa, and on to Pisa on the A12; via Lyons to Turin, then by the A21 and A26 to Genoa, and on to Pisa.

From Switzerland: via the Grand St Bernard Pass, and on to Genoa by the A5 and A26; via the St Gotthard or Simplon Passes to Milan, and by the A1 through Bologna.

From Austria: via the Brenner Pass and A22 (E6) through Modena.

Arriving

From Pisa airport there is a train service to Florence's Santa Maria Novella station, also called the Stazione Centrale; the journey takes about an hour. Buses leave Florence airport for the city centre, and the short journey is also feasible by taxi.

Long-distance buses cover

the whole of Tuscany, and there are frequent services from Florence to the rest of Tuscany. Contact the tourist office for full details of services (*see* **Tourist Information Offices**).

Within three days of arriving in Italy, all foreign nationals must register with the police. If you are staying in a hotel, the management will normally attend to this formality, but the visitor is responsible for checking that it has been carried out.

There is no limit on the importation into Italy of tax-paid goods bought in an EU country, provided they are for personal consumption, with the exception of alcohol and tobacco which have fixed limits governing them.

The fields turn yellow in summer with sunflowers.

A-Z

Accidents and Breakdowns

In the case of a breakdown, dial ☎ 116 from the nearest phone box and the operator will send an ACI (Italian Automobile Club) service vehicle. A red warning triangle should be placed 50m (55yds) behind the vehicle, and your hazard warning lights switched on. In the event of an accident, exchange names, addresses and insurance details. To contact the police or ambulance, dial ☎ 113. There are emergency telephones at 1km (0.6 mile) intervals along the *autostrade.*

Fully comprehensive insurance is advisable for motorists in Italy, and motoring organizations recommend that you carry a green card, although this is no longer a legal requirement. Should you need them, spare parts and service facilities for Italian makes of cars are simple to find, but all major towns have agencies for most other makes.

Accommodation

For information before you go on all aspects of staying in Tuscany, refer to the *Michelin Red Guide Italia.* The Italian government classifies hotels from one to five stars, and most towns in Tuscany are well supplied with accommodation in all classes, including guest houses (*pensioni*), and basic inns (*locande*). The average double bedroom with private bath/shower in a three-star hotel costs between 102 000 and 204 000 lire – less outside the main tourist areas.

Hotels located in popular tourist places are very much in demand, and it is advisable to reserve accommodation well in advance of your visit, particularly in the summer, or at Easter or Christmas.

There are a few youth hostels in the Tuscany region, namely in Florence and Lucca. For details of hostels and how to book, apply to The Italian Youth Hostel Association, Via Cavour 44, 00184 Rome.

The popular Kaffehaus, in the Boboli Gardens, Florence.

☎ 06 462 342. The youth hostel in Florence is at Federazione Italiana Alberghi per la Gioventù, Viale Augusto Righi 2, Firenze. Students' hostels also provide accommodation for young people in many towns, including Florence, Pisa and Siena.

There are many campsites in Tuscany, and details may be obtained by writing to: Federcampeggio, Castella Postale 23, 50041 Calenzano, Florence. ☎ 055 88 2391 (*see* **Camping**).

For information on accommodation and other aspects of your visit to Tuscany, contact the offices of the Italian State Tourist Offices (*see* **Tourist Information Offices**, p.125, for addresses and telephone numbers.)

Airports see **Arriving p.108**

Banks

Banks are open from 8.30am–1.30pm, Monday to Friday, and sometimes for one hour in the afternoon, usually 2.45–3.45pm. They are closed at weekends.

Tourists can change money at main railway stations and

airports, and travellers' cheques and cheques can be changed at most hotels, although the exchange rate may not be very favourable.

Beaches
There are resorts all along the Tuscan coastline, and many of them have sandy beaches and clean seas (*see* p.67).

Bicycles
Cycling is a popular way to get about in Tuscany, and there is no shortage of outlets hiring bikes to holidaymakers. Contact the Federazione Ciclistica Italiana, Piazza Stazione 2, Firenze.
☎ 055 283926

Books
Here are some suggestions to enhance your stay in Tuscany. Kenneth Clark's *Civilization*

remains a wonderful introduction to Western art; Chapter 4 'Man – the Measure of all things' is a splendid essay on the Italian Renaissance. Boccaccio's *Decameron* is still a cheerul, bawdy romp 600 years after it was written; or for more contemporary humour there is John Mortimer's *A Summer's Lease*. A more serious read for Tuscany – and the place where it was written – is Machiavelli's *The Prince*, an extraordinary book which laid the foundation of modern politics.

Breakdowns *see* Accidents

Camping
Italians love to go camping, and this is one of the most attractive areas for enjoying the outdoor life. The many sites range from the simple to the very sophisticated, and

Tuscany has a good range of lovely beaches.

prices vary accordingly. For full details of all the sites in this region apply to The Italian Camping Federation (Feder-campeggio), Casella Postale 23, 50041 Calenzano, Florence. ☎ 055 88 2391. Otherwise ask for information from the Italian Tourist Office in your own country (*see* **Tourist Information Offices**).

Car Hire

Florence, Siena and Pisa are quite well stocked with car-hire agencies, and there are outlets at Pisa airport, and Florence's main railway station (Santa Maria Novella) among other places. Airlines and tour operators offer fly/drive arrangements, and car hire in conjunction with train travel is also available through some of the major car hire companies.

Weekly rates with unlimited mileage offer the best deal; these include breakdown service and basic insurance, but you are advised to take out a collision damage waiver and personal accident insurance. The small local firms generally offer the cheapest rates, but they can only be booked locally. Most hire companies restrict hire of cars to drivers over 21.

Drivers must have held their full licence for at least a year. With the exception of Avis, there is an upper age limit of 60–65. Unless paying by credit card, a substantial cash deposit is required. Full details of the different hire schemes can be obtained from tourist offices. *See also* **Accidents and Breakdowns**, and **Tourist Information Offices**

Children

Italians adore children, and unfailingly enjoy taking them out to eat and being with them. Your children will be welcome virtually everywhere they go, and their behaviour will generally be tolerated. Baby food can be bought in chemists (*farmacia*), supermarkets and grocers.

Children under four not occupying a seat travel free on Italian railways; between the ages of four and 12, they get a reduction of 50 per cent. Babysitting can often be arranged by your hotel or *pensione*.

Churches *see* Religion

Climate *see* page 91

Clothing

Spring and autumn are warm and pleasant times of the year to visit Tuscany, and during those months light clothes can be worn in the day, with an extra sweater or jacket for the evenings and cooler days. The summer can be sweltering, especially when sightseeing in busy towns during July and August, when you will want to wear as few clothes as possible. Remember to cover up shoulders and upper legs when visiting churches.

Most Italian clothing measurements are standard throughout Europe but different from those in the UK and the US. The following are examples:

Dress Sizes

UK	8	10	12	14	16	18
Italy	38	40	42	44	46	48
US	6	8	10	12	14	16

Men's Suits

UK/US	36	38	40	42	44	46
Italy	46	48	50	52	54	56

Men's Shirts

UK/US	14	14.5	15	15.5	16	16.5	17
Italy	36	37	38	39/40	41	42	43

Men's Shoes

UK	7	7.5	8.5	9.5	10.5	11
Italy	41	42	43	44	45	46
US	8	8.5	9.5	10.5	11.5	12

Women's Shoes

UK	4.5	5	5.5	6	6.5	7
Italy	38	38	39	39	40	41
US	6	6.5	7	7.5	8	8.5

Complaints

Make any complaint at a hotel, shop or restaurant to the manager in a calm manner. For more serious complaints, contact the tourist office or threaten to involve the police, but be aware that a complaint to the latter can be very time-consuming. To avoid problems concerning overcharging, try to establish prices in advance, especially with taxi drivers and station porters. *See* **Tourist Information Offices**

Consulates

Embassies and consulates can be found at the following addresses:
British Consulate Via XX Settembre, 80a, 10122 Rome. ☎ 06 482 5441 **or** Lungarno Corsini 2, 50123 Florence. ☎ 055 28 4133 or 21 2594 **Irish Consulate** Largo del Nazareno 3, 00187 Rome. ☎ 06 678 2541 **Australian Embassy** Via Alessandria, 215, 00198 Rome. ☎ 06 83 2721 **Canadian Embassy** Via GB De Rossi 27, 00161 Rome. ☎ 04 44 5981 **New Zealand Embassy** Via Zara 28, Rome. ☎ 06 440 2928 **United States Embassy** Lungarno A Vespucci 38, 50123 Florence. ☎ 055 239 8276 **or** Via Veneto 119a, 00187 Rome, ☎ 06 467 41

Crime

As in many of the world's towns and cities, pickpockets operate in Tuscan towns, especially Florence, and muggers have been known to drive up on mopeds and grab handbags or wallets. The best advice is to be aware at all times, carry as little money and as few credit cards as possible, and leave any valuables in the hotel safe.

Carry wallets and purses in secure pockets inside your outer clothing, wear body belts, or carry handbags across your body or firmly under your arm. Never leave your car unlocked, and hide away or remove items of value.

If you have anything stolen, report it immediately to the police. Collect a report so that you can make an insurance claim. If your passport is stolen, report it to the Consulate or Embassy at once.

Currency see Money

Customs and Entry Regulations see Arriving p.108

Disabled Visitors

Tuscan towns, with their old buildings, ancient monuments and uneven roads and pavements, are not particularly suitable for disabled visitors,

Many wine cellars and shops offer tastings before you buy.

especially those confined to wheelchairs. Travellers are strongly recommended to check their particular requirements when making hotel or restaurant reservations.

Driving

Driving in Florence is difficult and frustrating, but having a car makes a lot of sense in Tuscany, and you will have complete access to the beautiful countryside of the region. Make sure that you are familiar with the rules of the road. Remember to drive on the right, and give way to traffic coming from the right – although you may notice that some Italian drivers take no notice of this rule.

Street parking is fraught with difficulties in most Tuscan towns, but there are official car parks which are secure and convenient, or you can leave the car on the outskirts of town and walk in or take a bus.

All of the main routes into towns and cities have petrol stations, and they are found at frequent intervals along motorways; they are normally open from 7.30am–noon, and 4.00–7.00pm, but opening hours vary, and depend on the season. Unleaded petrol is sold. Very few petrol stations accept credit cards.

Each section of the motorway (*autostrada*) requires payment of a toll; a card is collected when you enter the system and handed in when you leave, and a charge is made for the distance covered.

The following speed limits apply in Italy:
Cars and Motorcycles
Motorways 130kph/80mph (over 1100cc); 110kph/68mph (under 1100cc)
Country roads 90kph/56mph
Built-up areas 50kph/31mph
Campers
Motorways 100kph/62mph
Country roads 80kph/50mph
Built-up areas 50kph/31mph

Drivers should carry a full national or international driving licence, and an Italian translation of the licence unless it is a pink European licence; also insurance documents including a green card (no longer compulsory for EU members but strongly recommended), registration papers for the car, and a nationality sticker for the rear of the car.

Headlight beams should be adjusted for right-hand drive, and a red warning triangle must be carried unless there are hazard warning lights on the car; you should also have a spare set of light bulbs. The wearing of seatbelts is compulsory. *See also* **Accidents and Breakdowns**

Dry Cleaning see Laundry

Electric Current
The voltage in Italy is usually 220V. Plugs and sockets are usually round two-pinned ones, and adaptors are generally required.

Embassies see Consulates

Emergencies
In an emergency, for
Ambulance or **Police** ☎ 113
Fire ☎ 115
Red Cross Ambulance ☎ 5510
Traffic police (Florence) ☎ 352141
Stolen cars service (Florence)

☎ 49771

Automobile Club d'Italia
(car breakdown) ☎ 116

In cases of dire distress, the Consulate or Embassy might offer limited help.

Etiquette

As in most places in the world, it is considered polite and respectful to cover up decently in churches, museums, and theatres etc. Italians are a courteous people, and although less formal than many other Europeans, greet each other with good morning – *buon giorno*, or good evening – *buona sera*. This is usual when entering a restaurant, shop or hotel.

Excursions

Tuscany is famous for many things, not least the beautiful countryside that consists of hills and fertile valleys where the Chianti grape grows, and countless art treasures. There are organized tours of every description which do justice to all of these attractions, and details are usually available from your hotel or the tourist board (*see* **Tourist Information Offices**).

Guidebooks *see* **Maps**

Health

UK nationals should carry a Form E111 (forms available from post offices) which is

The main square, Pienza.

produced by the Department of Health, and which entitles the holder to free urgent treatment for accident or illness in EU countries. The treatment will have to be paid for in the first instance, but can be reclaimed later. All foreign nationals are advised to take out comprehensive insurance cover, and to keep any bills, receipts and invoices to support any claim.

Lists of doctors can be obtained from hotels, chemists (*farmacia*) or police stations, and first aid and medical advice is also available at pharmacies (look out for the red cross).

The latter are generally open from 9.00am–7.30pm, Monday to Saturday, with some variations, and lists of those which are open late or on Sundays are displayed at every chemist shop. The Farmacia at Santa Maria Novella railway station in Florence is open 24 hours. First aid (*pronto soccorso*) with a doctor is also available at airports and railway stations.

Hours see **Opening Hours**

Information see
Tourist Information Offices

Language
Most hotel staff, and sales personnel in the smart boutiques in places like Florence, Siena and Pisa, speak some English, but plenty of

---

Good morning / Buon giorno

Good afternoon/evening / Buona sera

Yes/no / Si/no

Please/thank you / Per favore/grazie

Do you speak English? / Parla inglese?

How much is it? / Quanto costa questo?

The bill, please / Il conto, per favore

Excuse me / Mi scusi

I'd like a stamp / Desidero un francobollo

Do you accept travellers' cheques? / Accetta travellers' cheques?

I don't understand / Non capisco

Italians do not understand the language. Your efforts to speak Italian will be much appreciated everywhere, and even a few simple words and expressions are often warmly received. Below opposite are a few words and phrases to help you make the most of your stay in Tuscany.

Laundry

Hotels charge high prices for laundry and dry cleaning, so it is well worthwhile finding a launderette where you can either do your own washing or have it done for you – there is no difference in the price. Florence has two day hotels with laundry facilities; ask your hotel for details, or enquire at the tourist office (*see* **Tourist Information Offices**).

Lost Property

Report any loss or theft to the police, or claim your possessions at Oggetti Ritrovati, Via Circondaria 19, Firenze. ☎ 367943 – open 9.00am– noon, Monday to Saturday. Airports and major railway stations have their own lost property offices, and if something goes missing in your hotel, check with the front desk and hotel security.

Should you lose any travel documents, contact the police, and in the event of a passport going missing, inform your Embassy or Consulate immediately (*see* **Consulates**).

Lost or stolen travellers' cheques and credit cards should be reported immediately to the issuing company with a list of numbers, and the police should also be informed.

Maps

A full range of maps and guides is published by Michelin. These include the *Motoring Atlas Italy*, Sheet Maps 988 (Italy) and 430 (Italy Centre), and the *Green Guide Italy*. Information on restaurants and accommodation can be found in the *Michelin Red Guide Italia*.

Medical Care *see* **Health**

Money

The monetary unit of Italy is the Italian lira, and notes are issued in denominations of 1 000, 2 000, 5 000, 10 000, 20 000, 50 000 and 100 000 lire. Coins are of 5, 10, 20, 50, 100, 200 and 500 lire. All major credit cards, travellers' cheques (American Express, Carte Bleue (Visa/Barclaycard), Diners Club and Eurocard (Mastercard/ Access) and Eurocheques are accepted in most shops, restaurants, hotels, and some large motorway petrol stations.

There are no restrictions on the amount of currency visitors can take into Italy, but perhaps the safest way to carry large amounts of money is in travellers' cheques which are widely accepted. Bureaux de change are found at airports, and larger railway stations, and at banks (*see also* **Banks**).

Exchange rates vary, so it pays to shop around. You are not advised to pay hotel bills in foreign currency or with travellers' cheques since the hotel's exchange rate is likely to be higher than that of the bureaux de change.

Newspapers

Foreign newspapers and magazines can be bought all over Tuscany from newsagents and kiosks. Florence's daily newspaper is *La Nazione*, and it carries information on summer activities for tourists, as well as details of entertainment and events. The free bilingual paper *Firenze Oggi/Florence Today* also has useful information.

Opening Hours

Shops are open from 8.30/9.00am–1.00pm, and from 3.30/4.00pm–7.30/8.00pm.

Many shops close all day on Sunday and on Monday morning, and sometimes on Wednesday afternoon.

Banks are open from 8.30am–1.30pm, and usually from 3.00–4.00pm.

Museums and galleries are mainly closed on Sunday afternoon and all day Monday. They are usually open from 9.00am–1.00/2.00pm, and sometimes from 5.00–8.00pm.

Post offices open 8.30am–2.00pm, Monday to Friday, and 8.30am–noon on Saturday.

Churches open at about 7.00am–noon, and from 4.00–7.00pm. The main churches are open all day.

Photography

Good-quality film and camera equipment are readily available but expensive in Tuscan towns. Before taking photographs in museums and art galleries you should check with staff as photography is sometimes restricted. Generally it is permitted in state-owned museums, although the use of flash and tripods is not, but you need special permission to film in municipal museums.

Police

The *carabinieri* deal with serious crime; the *polizia* handle general crime, including lost passports and theft reports for insurance claims; the *polizia stradale* handle traffic control outside towns; the *vigili urbani* deal with town traffic and adminis- tration. There are main police stations (*questura*) in the following towns:

Arezzo Via Fra' Guittone
Florence Via Zara 2
Lucca Viale Cavour 38

Daily shopping in the broad Piazza Dante, Grosseto.

Pisa Via M Lalli
Prato Via Valentini
Siena Via del Castoro

Post Offices

The main post office in
Florence is at Via Pellicceria,
off Piazza della Republica, and
is open 8.15am–7.00pm,
Monday to Friday, 8.15am–
1.00pm Saturdays. It provides a
24-hour international
telephone service, fax and
telex, as well as poste restante
facilities. Those collecting
poste restante mail should
bring their passport with them.

Otherwise post offices are
open 8.30am–2.00pm, Monday
to Friday, and 8.30am–noon on
Saturday. Stamps are sold only
by post offices, and tobacconists displaying a black and
white 'T' sign.

Public Holidays

New Year's Day: 1 January
Epiphany: 6 January
Easter Day and Easter Monday
Liberation Day: 25 April
Labour Day: 1 May
Assumption Day: 15 August
All Saints: 1 November
Immaculate Conception:
    8 December
Christmas Day & Boxing Day:
    25 & 26 December

Public Transport
see **Transport**

Church belfry, Montalcino.

Religion

English-language services are
held in Florence for the
following:
Catholic The Duomo, Saturday
5.00pm; a few other churches
celebrate mass in English, and
can give confession in English.
Church of England St Mark's,
Via Maggio 16.
American Episcopal St James',
Via B Rucellai, 9.
Christian Science Via della
Spada, 1.
Jewish Via Farini, 4.

Smoking

Smoking is banned in

churches, museums and art galleries, and is discouraged in restaurants. There are separate non-smoking compartments in trains.

Tobacconists (*tabacchi*), which carry a sign with a white 'T' inside a dark blue rectangle, sell the major international brands of cigarettes, which are also on sale in bars and restaurants.

Stamps see Post Offices

Taxis see Transport

Telephones

Italy is very well off for public telephones, which can be found on the streets, at railway stations and newsagents, and cafés and bars. These phones take telephone cards to the value of 5 000 or 10 000 lire, sold at newsagents and tobacconists, or 100, 200 and 500 lire coins, or tokens (*gettoni*). You can dial anywhere in Italy and abroad from these telphone boxes, but it is better to make international calls from main post offices, where you are charged at the end of your call.

To make an international call from Italy, dial 00 61 for Australia, 001 for US and Canada, 00 44 for UK, and 00 64 for New Zealand, then omit the first 0 of the city code. Cheap rates apply between 11.00pm–8.00am, Monday to Saturday, and all day Sunday.

Time Difference

Italian standard time is GMT plus one hour. Italian summer time begins on the last weekend in March when the clocks go forward an hour (the same day as British Summer Time), and ends on the last weekend in September when the clocks go back (one month before BST ends).

Tipping

A service charge of 10 or 15 per cent is usually included in the bill at hotels and restaurants in Italy, but a tip (minimum amount 1 000 lire) is also given where the service has been particularly pleasing. Check the bill to see if service has been included.

Usherettes who show you to your seat in a cinema or theatre should receive a tip, as should hotel, airport and railway porters, and lavatory attendants. Taxi drivers will expect about 10 per cent.

Toilets

There are toilets at most museums and galleries, theatres, airports and railway stations, restaurants and bars,

View through the trees to the tower of the Duomo, Lucca.

and usually large stores and shopping malls. Service stations on the *autostrade* always have facilities with toilets, and some ordinary petrol stations may have them too. Otherwise they are thin on the ground.

Toilets are often shared by the sexes, or they may be separate for women (*signore*) and men (*signori*).

Tourist Information Offices

The Italian State Tourist Office (ENIT) is a good source of information on what is happening in Tuscany, and the tourist information offices in the main Tuscan towns are as follows:

Arezzo Piazzale della Repubblica
Florence Via Cavour I/R, 50129 Firenze. ☎ 27 60 382
Lucca Via Vittorio Veneto 46
Pisa Palazzo Toscanelli
Siena Piazza del Campo

From here you can obtain information on timetables, accommodation and pro-grammes, and street plans. Most tourist offices publish a seasonal newsletter of what is on in their area.

Florence's official guide agency is Guide Turistiche, at Viale Gramsci 9a. ☎ 2478188. For information on visiting local farms and Chianti vineyards, contact Agriturist at

Piazza San Firenze, 3. ☎ 287838.

The tourist board also has offices in many countries, including the following English-speaking ones:
UK 1, Princes Street, London W1R 8AY. ☎ 0171 408 1254
USA 630 Fifth Avenue, Suite 1565, New York, NY 10111. ☎ 212 245 4822
Canada 1, Place Ville-Marie, Suite 1914, Montreal, Quebec, H3B 3M9. ☎ 514 866 7667/8/9
Australia and **New Zealand** ENIT, c/o Alitalia, Orient Overseas Building, Suite 202, 32 Bridge Street, Sydney, NSW 2000. ☎ 2 271 308
Eire 47 Merrion Square, Dublin 2. ☎ 01 766397

Tours see Excursions

Transport

Walking is probably the best way to see Tuscan towns since they are usually quite small and compact.

Information about travelling by **bus** in Florence, as well as tickets, can be obtained from the ATAF bus company office at Piazza del Duomo 57r. ☎ 212301. Main bus stations can also be found in the following towns:
Arezzo Viale Piero della Francesca

Lucca Piazza Verdi
Pisa Piazza Vittorio Emanuele
II and Piazza Sant'Antonio
Prato Piazza del Duomo
Siena Piazza San Domenico

Tickets for buses can also be bought in advance at tobacconists, bars and newspaper kiosks, and at automatic ticket machines at some main stops; books of tickets and passes are also available. Tickets should be stamped by a machine on boarding the bus, and on-the-spot fines are imposed if you do not have a validated ticket.

Frequent bus services also operate between Florence and the other towns of Tuscany, including Siena, Arezzo, Volterra, Lucca, Pisa, Prato and Pistoia. For details contact the various tourist offices.

Florence is linked to all of the main cities of Italy by a fast, reliable and inexpensive **railway** service, with trains arriving in the city at the Santa Maria Novella station. Various discounts can be taken advantage of, and there are five different categories of train with supplements chargeable for the fastest and most luxurious, so it is worth checking to get the best rates. There are also stations at Pisa, Lucca, Arezzo, Prato and Siena. For details of rail services throughout Tuscany, enquire at the tourist office.

Taxis can generally be found in special taxi ranks at railway stations and main squares of towns, and they can also be called by telephone:
Florence ☎ 4390 or 4798
Siena ☎ 49222 or 289350
Pisa ☎ 541600 or 41252
Fares are displayed on the meters, and there are extra charges for night service, Sundays and public holidays, luggage, and journeys outside town.

TV and Radio
There are no English-language television or radio broadcasts in the Tuscany region, but there are several TV and radio stations.

Vaccinations
see **Before You Go p.108**

Water
(drinking, shortage etc)
Tuscan water is safe to drink, although tap water in Florence does not have a very nice taste. Only where a tap has a sign saying *acqua non potabile* is the water not suitable for drinking. It is usual to order a bottle of water, *acqua minerale*, with meals.

Youth Hostels
see **Accommodation**

INDEX

FACTFINDER